BASIC BOOKS IN EDUCATION

Editor: *Kathleen O'Connor, B.Sc., Principal Lecturer in Education, Rolle College, Exmouth*
Advisory Editor: *D. J. O'Connor, M.A., Ph.D., Professor of Philosophy, University of Exeter*

Schooling in the Middle Years

Dance

Dance is much more than the random movements of the body. It can become an expressive art form through which pupils give shape to their thoughts and feelings about experience. It can all too easily be dismissed as a fruitless form of physical exercise, as Mr McKittrick is at pains to point out. In *Schooling in the Middle Years – Dance* the author analyses the basic skills of body control and describes how these can be harnessed to the purposeful expression of children's imaginations resulting in creative movement – dance.

Key words are in SMALL CAPITALS, there are summaries and 'further reading' lists at the end of each chapter and there is a full bibliography, glossary and index.

Schooling in the Middle Years

Dance

D. McKITTRICK
Senior Lecturer in Art of Movement
Goldsmiths' College, University of London

MACMILLAN

First published 1972

Published by
MACMILLAN EDUCATION LIMITED
Basingstoke and London

The Macmillan Company of Australia Pty Ltd Melbourne
The Macmillan Company of Canada Ltd Toronto
St Martin's Press Inc New York
Companies and representatives
throughout the world

Printed in Great Britain by
ROBERT MACLEHOSE AND CO LTD
The University Press, Glasgow

0035990
0-333-10924-4

793   374.
307   7933
MAC   MAC

TO EVELYN, AMANDA AND CHRISTOPHER

Contents

Acknowledgements   *page* 10

1   Some Reflections on Dance   11

2   Movement Material for the syllabus   24
    I In Action   24
    II Dynamic Action   36
    III Action in Space   44
    IV In Action Together   56
    V The Organisation by year of the Syllabus Content   69

3   The Roles of the Teacher   73

4   Making Dances   82

Bibliography   98

Glossary   100

Index   105

Acknowledgements

I am particularly indebted to Miss Simone Michelle, and Miss June Kemp of the Sigurd Leeder School of Dance for my education in dance.

My sincere gratitude also goes to Miss Joan Russell, Principal Lecturer in Dance at the Worcester College of Education, who guided my work there, deepened my understanding of the work of Rudolf Laban, and generously offered advice during the writing of the manuscript.

I am also grateful to Mr George McMurray for many long conversations, into the small hours, which have exercised such an influence on my views of dance in education.

I would also like to thank Miss Diana Jordan for reading the completed manuscript and making helpful suggestions leading to alterations and expansions.

I am grateful to my wife who read the manuscript in all of the stages of preparation and helped me to express my thoughts more clearly.

I am indebted to Mr Potter, Headmaster of Samuel Southall Secondary School, Worcester, and Mr Whyte, Headmaster of Christchurch C. of E. Primary School, London for opportunities to work with pupils in their schools and to take photographs of these pupils for the illustrations.

My thanks are due to the following for taking the photographs: Geoffrey N. Hopcraft of Worcester for plates 7, 8, 9, 10, 11, 12 and 13; Mrs Teena Newman of Hatfield, Broadoak for plates 5, 6, 16, 17, 18 and 19; Brian Walley of Worcester College of Education for 2, 3, 4, 14 and 15.

The extracts from *Dance and Drama in Bali* by Beryl de Zoete on pages 14, 18, 19, 21, 54 and 75 are reproduced with the permission of Faber & Faber.

1 Some Reflections on Dance

Clothes quickly pile up on the desks as children busily undress for the dance lesson. The first to change are soon by the door, ready to make their way to the hall, their bare feet wriggling impatiently in their shoes for the moment when they can kick them off and spring onto the hall floor. On the way along the corridor the bodies bustle and an animated walk threatens to break into running at any sign of indulgence from the teacher who tries to give a steady calm to the moment. Once inside the hall a line of shoes immediately appears under the chairs lined up along the wall and swift bare feet dart and prance in lively stepping and jumping. Some rush across the space exhilarated by the feel of the air against their faces, some pluck their feet off the floor in hops and leaps, and others swing wide their arms in unrestrained gesture which sweeps them high onto their toes, or pulls them into an off-balance suspension that dissolves into the slack of a downwards spiral. Soon the teacher calls for the class's attention and the lesson begins. When the lesson is over and these nine and ten year-olds leave the hall, an older class enters with a steady step. Two and three walk into the space after arranging their shoes under the chairs and begin working on a movement phrase. There is less of the exuberant leaping, stepping and whirling characteristic of the first class. Hands trace arabesque-like forms, feet brush the air, limbs unfold into the space and float or drift from one stillness to the next. Here and there two or three give up their conversations started in the corridor and link hands to step together, threading through the space in a line or enclosing the space in a circle.

These children are three or four years older than the nine and ten year-olds and in their dancing have not only preserved the rhythms of the younger age group, but have found a new range of movement which reveals the realms of feeling awakening within them. In addition to the accentuated twists, leaps, and steps characteristic of the nine and ten year-olds there is a more marked sense of power, a new lyricism animates the limbs which can move through the space with liquid smoothness or draw out lines in space with the tension of taut sinews.

All of these children are excited and involved in their work with a seriousness and absorption typical of classes who have a background of satisfying and memorable lessons. Such absorption as is described here grows out of a good teacher/class relationship combined with a wise choice of lesson material to meet the needs of each particular class. But in addition to teacher/class relationship and suitability of lesson content, there must be an intrinsic meaningfulness in the activity itself to sustain children's interest and absorption. The remainder of this chapter presents some reflections towards an understanding of the significance of dance. Only from such an understanding may its significance for children be appreciated.

The absorption with which children work in dance has been remarked upon by many teachers. What import can dance have to bring about such absorption? Observations made during classes give us many clues. When children dance we do not see bodies merely going through the actions of bending, stretching and twisting, or moving about by running and walking or some other form of locomotion. Such motor events as these, even when executed with good bodily management, are never dancing. Instead we see an arm drawn up into the air as if by some invisible thread, or a body caught in a spin as if by some whirlpool force. In these examples the movements appear to be reactions to external forces or influences and it is the children's intuitive perception of these illusory forces which perpetuates their absorption. The movement may not be in response to illusory *external* forces, however, for the force or influence may emanate from *within* in an act of will. In this case a child may sweep across the floor like a gust of wind, fly into the air with fists raised in an attitude of defiance; or restfully sink with a gesture of quiet acquiescence.

Such movement images create the illusion of influences or

forces and it is the interplay of such influences or forces which is revealed to the child when he dances and is presented to his imagination when he observes others in his class dancing. In this presentation of forces a dance reveals a part of subjective life. The body becomes the instrument through which felt energies play out their rhythms in *forms* symbolic of the life of feeling.

In dancing the life of feeling is given objectivity in precise and manageable structures. Every dance is susceptible to the child's control. He may draw out one part and curtail another; change the point of climax from the middle to the end, repeat a section to add emphasis, alter the accentuation to bring about a new pattern or increase the duration of a pause to heighten the effect of a subsequent swift moving phrase.

The significance of dance as the objectivisation of life forces in manageable forms is confirmed by taking a historical perspective. Though the view, preserved by records, of dancing in early cultures is incomplete, the dances of those peoples who still exist help us to fill out the gaps in the picture.

The primitive's most vivid and intense apprehension of forces arose from his inner world where desire, the source of energy, charged his bodily action and gave rise to his first sense of efficacy as an independent being. Ernst Cassirer in the *Philosophy of Symbolic Forms*, Vol. II, quotes F. W. Schelling (3, p. 8).

It is not with things that man has to do in the mythological process, it is powers arising within consciousness itself that move him.

In early cultures the primitive's experience of power within the body was both given form and recognised in sacred images such as animal sculptures and masks, but the most immediate image to embody that power was the dynamic image of the dance. Curt Sachs, the scholarly historian of the dance and music, refers to the expression of powers in dance. He writes in *World History of the Dance* (35, p. 4).

Repressed powers are loosed and seek free expression.

Herbert Read also recognises the containment of powers within the art form. He writes in *Icon and Idea* of the existence of space as a mystery in the human consciousness (p. 11). Space, he says,

... was a nothingness out of which all imaginable powers could emerge. Some of these powers might be beneficient, others destructive, but all alike had to be propitiated. The work of art became an act of containment and propitiation.

Susanne Langer sees powers more specifically as the primary creation of dance. In *Feeling and Form*, where she sets out her theory of art, she writes (19, p. 189):

The dance creates an image of nameless and even bodiless Powers filling a complete autonomous realm, a 'world', it is the first presentation of the world as a realm of mystic forces.

From these authors we learn that the savage gives form to vitality itself by the creation of the appearance of powers. Dances which show these powers in interaction may be found today in many parts of the world. On the island of Bali, for instance, the dances of the Barong and Rangda are still performed. Beryl de Zoete in *Dance and Drama in Bali* gives authoritative accounts of these impressive dances and comments on their symbolic nature. The Barong and Rangda are two monster figures. Each of these figures is composed of a huge mask with many colourful, ornate, and complex trappings and requires two dancers to animate it. The creature's costume is like our pantomime donkey in that it completely conceals the dancers, but where the donkey's repertoire is relatively limited, the movement repertoire of the Balinese Barong and Rangda includes an extensive range of expressive gestures and steps. The nature of their dance is defined by Beryl de Zoete (4, p. 97).

The real drama of the Barong play begins with the entry of Rangda ... in a crescendo of magic power. There is not necessarily any story other than the symbolic encounter of two great forces, both inimical to man, but one of which he has succeeded in winning to his side.

The Barong monster is described by her as ... 'a protagonist of men against the dark intruding death-force of Rangda'.

In all of these dances of the Barong and Rangda the magic powers which are apprehended in the Balinese consciousness are given external form. The dance is the very embodiment of these powers and in its progression shows their interplay.

Dancing as it is represented in our society today is as much a play of powers as ever it was in history, but it is obvious that it differs in one essential factor. The powers loosed in the primitive dance were believed to be real whereas they are now recognised as the illusory creation of the dance.

It is the act of creating the semblance or illusion of an interplay of powers which separates dance from the everyday level of movement to an elevated level of art where movement no longer serves any utilitarian aim. Children are unable to verbalise on this distinction between the illusory realm of art and the realm of day-to-day living, but we may be sure that this distinction is vividly clear to their intuitions.

A child of mine was asked, 'What is dancing'. 'I don't know', she said. 'What do you think it is?', the questioner persisted. 'Well', she replied, 'it's not everyday movements'. Teachers know how readily children recognise the transformation which ordinary materials undergo in art. In drawing, for example, children take pleasure in the transformation which mere lines and shapes undergo as form emerges with all the semblance of animation, taking the appearance of living beings in illusory space. The drawing of 'The Ballerina' (plate 1) illustrates how lines can create this illusion of a living presence in illusory space.

The significance of artefacts such as dances, paintings, and sculptures is expressed through the illusions peculiar to each. In dancing there are three illusions created. There is the primary illusion which may be named by the words 'powers', 'forces', or 'influences', and the secondary illusions of space and time. A brief consideration of how each of these illusions is created in dancing will help the reader to approach the chapters which follow with greater insight.

THE ILLUSION OF POWERS

EFFORT, a technical word, in the context presented here, referring to the quality of movement, is particularly important in the creation of the illusion of powers. It is to the insight of Rudolf Laban that we owe the concept of effort presented in Chapter 2 II. Laban recognised the importance of effort in the manifestation of powers and saw the origins of such manifestations in religious dances. In *The Mastery of Movement* (16, p. 18), he writes:

In religious dances man represented those superhuman powers which, as he conceived, directed the happenings of Nature and determined his personal and tribal fate. He gave physical expression to certain qualities he noted in the actions of these superhuman powers.

And later (p. 156) when speaking of the dancer's abstract compositions, he writes:

Dance is for these artists a manifestation of those inner forces out of which the complications of human happenings grow.

An understanding of effort is clarified by looking at its aspects in turn and in each case considering the contribution of that aspect to the creation of this primary illusion. Each aspect of effort is referred to as a MOTION FACTOR. There are four motion factors; namely *weight, flow, time* and *space*.

Each of these factors will now be considered in turn.

The motion factor of weight

The attitude of the child to the motion factor of weight is revealed by the degree of force shown in his movement. This force may be exerted all at once or grow gradually. Whether the illusory powers created by dance appear as strong or weak depends on the degree of tension exerted by the child in his dancing. An infinite variety of movements may be visualised. In moments of delicate tension the limbs may lift and fall, drawing out forms in space with the fragility of the finest silken threads. In moments of great tension the body may be pulled to the limit of extension or crushed into a huddled form. Between these two extremes lie many dynamic nuances.

The motion factor of flow

The child's attitude to the motion factor of flow is revealed by the degree of control shown in his movement. This may vary from abandon to restraint and the choice will influence the fluency with which the apparent powers operate. Abandoned power will be created in movement where the arms fly out repeatedly in a cascade of gesture as the body spirals upwards. Restrained power will be created when the body rises up steadily, while the arms carefully open to the side as though they drew apart curtains upon a landscape. Between these two contrasting expressions lie many dynamic nuances.

The motion factor of time

The child's attitude to the motion factor of time is revealed either in a degree of leisure or a degree of haste. The illusory powers created will be experienced as sustained or swift depending on which attitude the child takes. In the former the body may drift languidly in a spirit of rest while in the latter one darting action may be piled upon another in a shower of urgent gesticulations. Between these two contrasting dynamics many nuances of expression exist.

The motion factor of space

The child's attitude to the motion factor of space is revealed by the manner in which the movement evolves in space varying from indirectness at one extreme to directness at the other. In the former case power will appear to undulate through the body or be diffused throughout the whole body so that the movements evolve in space with pliancy, and in the latter case power will appear directly so that the limbs move with singleness of intent. It would be wrong to imagine that only one factor dominates in dance for it is equally possible for two factors to be of equal importance in the child's consciousness. The weight factor and the flow factor could both be important for example, and the dance would then show the play of tension and flow.

The second illusion created in dancing is the illusion of space and it is to it that we now turn.

THE ILLUSION OF SPACE

The connotation of the word space in this context is to be carefully distinguished from the connotation of the same word in the context of effort. In this context space connotes form and refers to the shapes and patterns created in movement whereas in the context of effort the connotation of space is the dancer's attitude to space.

The actual room or spatial area in which the dance takes place is quite distinct from the illusory space created by the dance itself. This latter space may be moulded in many ways, some of which are described in the following paragraphs.

An infinite extent may be given to the dance space by movement in which big sweeping curves and broad swinging arcs just skim the ground and soar into the air above the head, or long gestures which extend out from the body into the space, seeming to stretch further than is possible because of the distant focus in the eyes and the supporting alignment of the rest of the body. At the other extreme the curve of the body and close ranging compass of the eyes and gestures may so curtail the reach of the movements as to give the impression of a diminished space.

In a sense the dance space created is a kind of architecture whose line, angles, and forms are left in the memory as movement succeeds movement. Sinuous gestures spin a meandering thread which creates a labyrinthine tracery of curves while directed jumps zigzagging from one precise point to another create an angular pattern broken up into segments. As a dance grows, so specific areas seem to emerge and become so firmly fixed in the imagination that the dancer feels as though he may step out of one and enter another. When the body spreads wide on both sides with spatial clarity then an imaginary wall is created which divides the space in front from the space behind. Repetition of this motif would plant the image firmly enough in the imagination so that the dancer could use the areas on each side of the wall. Another movement motif may create an illusion of a roof under which the dancer can shelter, or a corridor along which he travels.

The possibilities multiply considerably when there is more than one person. A vivid description of 'dance space' is presented by Beryl de Zoete in *Dance and Drama in Bali* (4, p. 230). This dance episode is part of the Legong dance.

. . . the penaser sang and upon this song he seemed to weave his dance. There was a pathetic pause during which his height unfolded till his body appeared gigantic. The two did a marvellous duet, the penasar dancing at the level of Civa's knees, which gave the impression of gigantic height to Civa, almost as if his body were in the clouds and his feet alone belonged to earth.

The second of the subsidiary illusions created by dance is time and it is to a consideration of this illusion that we now turn.

THE ILLUSION OF TIME

The illusion of time has to do with change or growth, the organic aspect of dance. Every movement is seen within a context of past, present, and future.

Some movements give the impression of holding on to the past or trying to prolong the past because the dancer's focus of attention remains on the beginning of the movement while the middle passes as if unnoticed. Other movements appear to hasten to the future because the dancer's focus of attention points to the end of the movement so that the beginning and middle stage appears to pass unmarked. When every stage is given equal attention then the appearance of experiencing the present to the full is created.

Another aspect of time which is part of the illusory schema is pace or rate of progression. The sense of progression which is built up may be made either to increase or decrease by either rapidly or gradually realising the potential development felt in each phrase. Here it is not a case of mere succession of one movement by another but of the greater or lesser degree of urgency felt to be latent in each part of the dance, an urgency which leads to expectancy of some conclusion. The expected future which the dance engenders may be held in suspense. This happens when our expectations are aroused and then denied the cadence which is anticipated. It is by gradually developing the ability to build dance sequences that control of the illusion of time is achieved.

The preceding paragraphs put forward the view of dance as a creation of the illusion of powers in equally illusory space and time. The significance of dance lies in its presentation of the interplay of powers and it is through this interplay that the life of feeling is revealed.

It is now appropriate to consider how the significance or import of a dance may be appreciated and the value of such appreciation in the process of educating feeling.

THE APPRECIATION OF DANCE IMPORT AND THE EDUCATION OF FEELING

When the imagined feeling which is formulated by a dance becomes clear it is a natural urge to want to communicate what we have understood of this formulation of feeling. Words are the usual mode of such communication and such words as playful, humorous, joyful, lyrical, dramatic, powerful, fantastic, heroic, fearful, and so on might enter into such a communication. But any such attempt to communicate the import of a dance to others is bound to fail, for the real import of the dance is inseparable from the dance itself. It might be thought that this import of the dance form is nebulous and imprecise since it defies translation into words. In fact, two commentaries about the same dance might support this assumption by their dissimilarity. However, the lack of congruence in the commentaries arises not from any vagueness in the dance, which is exact in its import, but from the unsuitability of words to deal adequately with the subjective realities revealed clearly in the dance. The development of the child's appreciation of the import of dance forms is a fundamental objective in dance education.

The education of feeling through dance is a gradual process marked by moments of insight which may occur almost simultaneously with a dance experience or after a long period of consolidated experience. The flow of movement punctuated by pauses and longer stillnesses is a fundamental experience in this education. In fact the very sense of being alive is intensified by the rhythms felt in the flow of movement. The activities of improvising, remembering and repeating improvisations, and working over improvisations to perfect them are all part of the process of dance education. In addition, observation of the improvisations and finished dance sequences of others followed by discussion helps to bring new shades of meaning to the practical work.

Movement itself is suitable subject matter to inspire the above activities. Such subject matter might include bodily actions such as jumping and stepping, turning and twisting, and gesturing; movement qualities such as smooth and sharp or sudden and sustained; spatial ideas such as big and small; or high and low and ideas involving partners such as meeting and parting.

In the Middle School, however, where easy passage from one subject area to another is part of the educational goal, many activities which the children pursue in the sciences, the humanities and the other arts will produce ideas and material usable in dance improvisations and compositions. But whatever the subject matter from which the exploration takes its inspiration, a suitable abstraction of some feature of the subject must be made in terms of bodily action. The snake, for example, with its distinctive movements may be taken as a subject for movement exploration. No literal imitation of the reptile's movement is possible but by an appropriate selection from his repertoire of bodily action a dance phrase can be found which abstracts those features in the snake which the child finds significant. In this abstraction the body may shift sinuously from one position to another, the eyes may peer, fixing an imaginary focus, and the head may rear as the body poises on the toes which holds the floor with a ready tension. Here, something of the rhythms and undulating movement of the snake may be captured, the imperceptible changes of position in which sustainment is dissolved into stillness or broken by unexpected swiftness. It is in the appropriate use of the body's repertoire of movement that the abstraction of significant features is effected. The Balinese are particularly ingenious in using the animal as subject. The following passage is from *Dance and Drama in Bali* (4, p. 278). Beryl de Zoete describes fragments from their animal dances. The choice of bodily action is clear in each fragment.

... the slow rocking hops and curious pushing steps, accompanied by quick circling glances of Nala and Singa, the lions, the wide springs with two feet together of Goaksa and Vinata, the birds, the little zigzagging steps and high rising on toes with a sigh, the coy twisting springs and furtive gestures of Harina and Menda, the deer, the stealthy steps with high raised feet, pauses, curves and peering glances of Bawimoeka and Asiboda, the dog and pig, the curvetting step and rearing neck of Droea, the snake, and the dipping role of Asti, the elephant.

Regardless of the subject matter inspiring dance, there are two kinds of insight into the life of feeling that the child gains from dancing. In one, feelings already vaguely felt and frequently undergone are given form in some new dance experience. In the other, areas of feeling never before experienced are discovered in a dance form. Both of these experiences of insight are a necessary part of the education of feeling and it is in the accumulation of such insights that the conceptual value of dance lies. In life we undergo feeling, think about it and talk about it but since feeling cannot be conceived in the mode of words, another mode is required. That mode is art; and in dancing, the art form whose medium is the most immediate of all to the child, the real conception of feeling may grow. In *Icon and Idea*, Herbert Read goes further in his claims for the function of art. He writes (29, p. 105):

... the purpose of art is not to expend feeling, or excite feeling, but rather to give feeling form, to find its 'objective correlative', so that we may recognise it for what it is, for what it signifies in our discourse. Art is always the instrument of consciousness as apprehension, realisation, materialisation.

Middle Schools cater for pupils in either the age range 8 – 12, or 9 – 13, during which years childhood ends and adolescence begins. In these years which see such significant growth in personality no area of the curriculum which contributes to the education of feeling, as dance does, can afford to be neglected.

SUMMARY

1. Dance is more than rhythmic movement; it is a way of moving which creates the illusion of powers, in equally illusory space and time.
2. Through the progression of movement experienced in dance sequences, the play of these illusory powers is presented.
3. Dance is a significant activity in education because it gives form to feeling.
4. The child gains insight into feeling through the development of his appreciation of dance forms.

FURTHER READING

Langer (19): The whole of Part 1, Chapters 11 and 12 of Part 2, and the whole of Part 3 are essential reading for a good understanding of the nature of dance as an art form.

Langer (20): Chapters 6 and 7 trace the role of dance in the evolution of sacrament and myth.

Langer (20): Chapters 9 and 10 should be read in considering 'meaning' in connection with the arts.

Langer (21): A most readable book which will contribute to the reader's understanding of dance in education.

Langer (22): Chapter 1 is an essay on dance. Chapter 2 clarifies the meaning of the term 'expressiveness'. Chapter 3 is interesting and informative on the subject of creativity.

Read (28) and Cassirer (3) both show the role of art in the development of human consciousness.

Jordan (13) presents a clear introduction to dance in education.

Laban (17): Chapter 1 gives an historical perspective of dance in education.

Russell (32): Chapter 2 considers dance in the Middle School.

North (23): The introduction is an authoritative statement on movement education.

2 Movement Material for the syllabus

I IN ACTION

One of the teacher's aims in every dance lesson will be to give the child an experience of being caught up in a rhythmic flow of movement. This can be achieved by stimulating and guiding movement improvisation and exploration on the basic bodily actions of stepping, travelling, turning, jumping, contracting, extending and gesturing. In this improvisation and exploration the child learns to bind the flow of movement by hesitation, pausing and stopping, and to free the flow of movement by allowing the action to unfold in an unhampered way. Stopping arrests the flow of movement completely and results in stillness. A good control of stillness is important since it enables the child to make a clean start and finish to each phrase of movement. Rhythmic phrases result from the simple task of 'going and stopping'. Travelling is a useful activity for 'going and stopping'. One half of the class can close its eyes and listen to the pattern of sound made by the running feet of the other half. Rhythmic pattern can also be made by beating the hands on the floor. Repeating a travelling and stopping activity gives the child the contrasting experience of energy spent in going and energy contained in stopping. In travelling there is a journey to be made from one spot to another and as a result there is a destination. In stepping, however, the emphasis is on the nature of the steps taken. The steps may be whole steps or half steps. We use whole steps in everyday walking when the feet pass each other and the weight of the body is transferred alternately from one foot to the other. Only in arriving or stopping do we bring our feet together to take the weight.

Half steps are made when from a 'feet together' position we

take a step into a feet-apart position, or when from a feet-apart position we take a step to make a feet-together position.

Exploration of half steps and whole steps is an important part of building movement vocabulary. Sequences entirely composed of whole steps have a free and unrestricted expression whereas sequences entirely composed of half steps have a halting expression. Where both kinds of steps are included in sequences, there is scope for numerous rhythmic variations. Half steps and whole steps used together as a lesson theme, however, are usually more successful when introduced to experienced and/or older classes, which are experienced in the fundamental work considered earlier in this chapter.

Repeated very short durations of lively travelling or stepping will enliven a class and this animation will be noticeable in their faces. It is important to balance this vigorous action with a more calming action to avoid overexciting the class. In travelling and stepping the child's focus is constantly changing. One minute his front is towards one part of the room and the next towards another.

In contrast, actions on the spot tend to keep the same front and thereby make for a static feeling. An on-the-spot activity like contracting and extending will therefore calm the class after an exciting activity like energetic travelling or stepping. Travelling tends, figuratively speaking, to shake up and diffuse one's concentration, while gathering the parts of one's body together by contracting helps to centre concentration. Contracting and extending are movements basic to life. William James (12, p. 372) wrote:

The tendency to contract is the source of all the self-protective impulses and reactions which are later developed, including that of flight. The tendency to expand splits up on the contrary into the impulse and instincts of an aggressive kind.

Contracting seems to have a comforting sensation for children and the above quotation goes some way towards explaining the reason.

When the child's attention is drawn to parts of the body involved in contracting and the question is asked whether these parts all begin moving simultaneously and stop simultaneously or whether they move one after the other, then exploration is encouraged and more variation in response is obtained. As the body is symmetrical other variations lie in the possibilities of one side contracting first or contracting more than the other side. It is important to remember at this point that the individual responses of each child are only going to leave a lasting impression if he has an opportunity to repeat his response often enough to remember it.

An action which will make a contrast to the more static nature of contracting and extending is jumping. Jumping satisfies childrens' liveliness. Real enjoyment in jumping grows out of security in using the floor. Only after establishing a confident step and a firm stance will children experience the full exhilaration of jumping in the dance lesson. This applies particularly to the early experience of the age groups of 13 and over. Words and phrases like 'flying', or 'shooting into the air', or 'snatching the body up off the floor' are helpful in stimulating elevation. By the time children reach their second year in the middle school, that is at the age of 9 or 10, airborne jumps should be well established within their movement vocabulary.

The experience of feeling suspended at the height of a leap contrasts with the feeling of being rooted in the ground in deep firm stances. It is interesting to note that the classical ballet, which arose in the courts of Italy and France, specialises in elevating movements which aim to defy gravity, while the dance of Bali, Java, Ceylon, India and Japan is noted for its movements which are rooted in the ground. In dance education elevated movement and deep-rooted movement are equally important.

Many children's games consist of skipping and hopping. Hopscotch is an example. A hopping game in which a ball on a string tied to one ankle is swung centrifugally while the other foot hops high enough to allow the string to pass underneath in its gyrations has had long seasons of recent popularity. Hopping is a static jump which belongs to the spot and has an up-down character. Skipping is a fluent form of hopping. A take-off from two feet and a landing on one makes for an airborne jump. In jumping from one foot and landing on two the take-off is weaker unless assisted by a travelling preparation and the broader base provided by the two-feet landing gives an earthy feeling to the jump. In jumping from one foot to the other, especially with travelling transitions, each jump covers the ground horizontally and has a feeling of expansiveness and freedom. Repeated jumps make rhythmic patterns and in any phrase of movement a single jump will make a good climax point. To be enjoyed at its best, jumping should not be carried on too long and needs a lot of space. Jumping excites children and needs sensitive handling if concentration is to be kept and expressiveness not to give way to mere acrobatic display. For all children, however, the vital experience in jumping is the contrast between being rooted or earth-bound and being airborne. Elevation can be experienced, of course, without jumping, by rising on the balls of the feet, and in this action the feeling of elevation will be intensified if the chest is uplifted.

In jumping the variations and shades of expression are numerous. Whether the focus of the eyes is upwards or downwards, for example, is significant and the teacher should try to take note of this feature during lessons in which elevation is a theme. Such questions as 'Which part of the body is highest?', 'What does your body do in the air? Does it spread, extend, contract, or turn?' will encourage awareness and may be asked while the class is in action.

Turning is as common an everyday action as travelling. We are constantly turning to focus on new points of interest. We turn to face our friends, and we turn to avoid a collision. We may turn on the spot, making a quarter, half or whole turn, or may make several turns. We may hesitate during a turn and then turn back to our starting place again. We may turn only the head to focus on a point or, if our whole attention is required, we may bring the whole body to face this point. A more subjective kind of turning occurs when we turn solely to experience the sensation of turning. You will have noticed children spinning round and round till they fall down in fits of laughter. Their arms fly out with the centrifugal force which gathers in the spinning. Whirling is a version of turning in which force is given to the action by rapid stepping on the spot or gathering and strewing arm gestures. In crowded places in everyday life we turn to avoid bumping.

Children enjoy weaving in and out of the spaces when they are travelling quickly. The quick and frequent changes of direction during this activity encourage bodily mobility. There is already a rich store of material for lessons in the actions which have been considered so far, but when it is recognised that bodily actions can be combined, so that, for example, a turn is executed while extending or contracting, or a jump is done with a turn, the possibilities seem endless. It is partly due to the limitless scope for individual interpretation in bodily action that the dance teacher continually sees original and pleasing responses to tasks he has set over and over again. While it is important to encourage the participation of the whole of the body in bodily actions, it is a further development of awareness to be able to emphasise particular body parts in an action. The rest of this chapter will deal with activities which foster this awareness.

One of the easiest parts of the body to stress is the feet. Children can improvise on the possibilities of bringing different parts of the feet into contact with the floor. Activities such as little bouncing jumps on the balls of the feet are possible in this exploration. Many sequences will arise from stepping on heels and toes. The teacher can use verbal accompaniments such as 'heel, heel, toe, toe, heel, heel, toe, toe' or 'toe, toe, toe, toe, heel, heel, toe, toe, toe, toe, heel, heel'. The heels and toes may be kept near the floor in these sequences or one foot may lift off the floor in a preparatory gesture prior to contact with the floor. The whole body may lift with this gesture and sink with a deep bend in the supporting leg as the gesturing foot descends. The foot may dart out in a quick gesture, with the ball of the foot touching the floor a little way off from the point of support and the body may then be taken on to the new spot marked by the gesturing foot to hover there. From a fixed spot on the floor the foot may dart out and then snap back in again to stillness beside the supporting foot. Many sequences will arise from such explorations and in the right atmosphere comic or dramatic dances readily result. In an ordinary walk the parts of the foot touch the floor in sequence, but in stamping all parts touch simultaneously.

Gripping, releasing, smoothing and cutting are examples of actions which will be helpful in stimulating improvisation on hand gestures. When the hands are in close proximity they may move so that the edges touch and part. Palms can face each other or rotate away from each other. The top and bottom of the knuckles can lead the hand in undulating action. The action of the hands can be made to influence the whole body. For example, if a hand rotation is continued past the normal degree, the shoulder and then the trunk will be involved. This action-play will result in unusual knotted body shapes which the child may be encouraged to unravel expressively. The rhythm created by gesture differs significantly from that of the feet. The heart and feet set a metrical rhythm which is measurable but the freer rhythm of breathing and gesture set a rhythm which is not.

Metrical rhythm is characterised by a periodicity and repetition which leads to a familiar pattern. Feeling or seeing the beginning of the pattern often enables the conclusion to be anticipated. Folk dance steps are in metrical rhythms. The pulse set up in metrical steps is quite regular and measurable and its steady character invites our foot-tapping response or hand clapping. Free rhythm is more complex and not given to the periodicity of metrical rhythms. Movements merge with each other in such a way that the end of the first movement may be the preparation for the second. The movements will often be of different lengths and there need be no repetition or periodicity. Breathing is an example of free rhythm.

In gesture particular parts of the hand may be emphasised. The palms can smooth and the finger tips poke, stab and penetrate space. The thumb edge of the hand, and the little finger edge can initiate slicing or cutting movement. The fists can pound the air and the palms can slap the thighs or knees. The palm of one hand can make a surface for the back or palm of the other hand to slap. The back of the clenched fist can push away the air. This produces a powerful movement when the whole body is involved. The palms of the hands can move in unison to make rebuffing actions, smoothing, patting, and stroking actions. This hand play is a very rich source of movement invention, particularly when the child is encouraged to let the body act sympathetically with the action of the hand. Children can create short dramatic and serious conversations or playful and comic ones. Children may absorb their movement experiences into wider intellectual activity. The movement in certain situations clearly becomes pantomimic, but the literal association of the pantomime should be swallowed by the forms and rhythms which are the end product in dancing.

The child's awareness of elbows and knees may also be developed in the early dance experiences. The knees can play a leading part in skipping jumps by shooting into the air and in this way helping the whole body to get off the ground. When the knees reach into space around the trunk grotesque body shapes result. Strong, slow gestures of this kind have a dramatic character whereas suddenness and delicacy lend an impish and mischievous expression to these movements. Knees and elbows may approach each other, touch and part. In elbow-knee conversations of this kind there is great scope for movement imagination. Play concerned with the proximity of knees and elbows is at first more successful in a slow tempo. Afterwards, when judgement of the distance involved and the co-ordination required are practised, the tempo may be quickened. The ways in which the knees and elbows meet will vary, depending on which joint is the more active. The knees may be still while the elbow approaches. Both elbows or one only may approach. The right elbow may approach the left knee. In this case the body becomes more twisted and asymmetric in shape. Further exploration is possible when the theme concerns the proximity of the elbows and knees to the floor. As with earlier mentioned bodily action, gestures of hands and feet, elbows and knees may be combined with other actions. For example, the elbow may lead the whole body into a turn, leap, extension or contraction.

Wrists and ankles correspond in the same way as elbows and knees. Leading movement with the wrists and ankles is not as easy as leading with the elbows or knees. The ornamental style of Restoration court movement owed its character to the great play of the wrists in the gestures of people at court, and in the manipulation of the fan. Movement play greatly involving the wrist often reflects this style. It is, of course, not at all childlike. Gestures led by the wrists or ankles such as wrists meeting and parting sometimes appeal to adolescent girls. Boys are happier when the stress is on knees and hands.

It is a sign of progress when children can get caught up in a flow of action initiated by elbows, knees or hands and involving the action of leaping, travelling and turning. This fluency demands good body co-ordination and would not be expected of an inexperienced class. Transitions between leaping and travelling require skill which is only acquired gradually. Eleven-year-olds with two years' dance experience may achieve this fluency.

So far the bodily actions of travelling, contracting and extending, jumping, turning and stopping have been considered. In these actions the need to encourage the participation of the whole body was recognised. After this, activities which develop awareness of the extremities, and the elbows and knees were examined. Now it is time to look closely at activities which in particular involve the trunk. The trunk needs as much work as the limbs if it is to be as mobile and as expressive as the rest of the body. By adolescence some children already find it uncomfortable to sit on the floor without the helping support of the hands or elbows. Dance work must help to preserve into adulthood the bodily plasticity and mobility characteristic of children's movement. Although, through exploring bodily action and working at their own compositions, children will have opportunities for developing the mobility of the trunk, the teacher must be able to observe when trunk awareness is lacking and know the kind of actions to choose in order to improve this awareness. The rest of this chapter will examine such actions.

Gesture is an important action in this connection. In gesture the flow of movement may be sequential or simultaneous. In simultaneous body flow, all the body parts involved start moving at the same time and finish moving at the same time. When they start one after the other and stop one after the other, the flow is sequential. Sequential movements involving the whole body create a wave-like action. Such actions are particularly effective in promoting trunk mobility. The wave can start in one part of the body and flow through to another. For example, it can begin in the knee and travel through the pelvis, waist, chest and head in turn. It may be in a forwards or sidewards direction. It may begin in the hip area and flow through waist, chest, shoulder, elbow, wrist and hand or begin in the hip area and flow through the knee and foot. These waves can be done in standing, sitting, kneeling or lying positions. Children will respond to the task 'See if you can make a wave flow through every part of your body' by finding some of the above sequences for themselves.

Another action which helps promote awareness in the trunk is stepping. Certain kinds of stepping bring the hips into action. For example, a side step where one foot crosses over the other brings the hip region into a twisted position. If we take the right foot as an example, it can step to the side either by crossing in front of the left foot or by crossing behind. Travelling motifs where the side steps alternate from crossing in front to crossing behind bring about hip twists or rotations which alternate in direction with each step. These motifs provide opportunities for children to develop awareness in the hip region. Exploration could include varying the degree of hip rotation, the level of the stepping from deep steps, in which the knees are brought fully into play, to high steps, in which the knee action is at a minimum. Once this travelling motif is mastered the steps could develop into step-and-jump motifs, in which the twists lead into complete turns.

Extra large steps may also include the hip region whatever the step direction might be. The exaggerated extensions in large steps bring the whole body into deep situations near the floor. Motifs consisting of this kind of stepping bring about expressions of a grotesque or powerful character partly because of the body shape which results and partly because of the strength required.

It is important, at this point, to remember that along with the development of bodily action, the child's appreciation of stillness must grow. Four kinds of stillness may be described. The first is the end position or finishing position. This stillness will often take a kneeling, sitting or lying position which may be either the settled rest and calm after a phrase of action involving elevation, or a contracted position which may be the conclusion of a fine-spun phrase that weaves from the periphery of the body to the body centre. Stable stances in which the feet take sure hold on the floor will also occur frequently as final positions. The movement which leads to these positions will often include asymmetric forms of travelling and jumping which need the steadying influence of symmetry to bring about a controlled conclusion. The second stillness is experienced in positions which are the spring-board for action. In this state of readiness there is the alertness and tension preceding the release of energy. It is recognisable in the grip before the release, the crouch on the ground before the release, the crouch on the ground before the spring into space, the twist before the turn, the holding back before the advance, the high stance before the descent, the contraction before the explosion. The third stillness occurs in that in between state experienced as suspension. It may be the moment between the crest of the leap and the fall, the moment between the end of the swing out and the swing in, or the hesitation or pause punctuating a movement phrase. The fourth stillness exists as an attempt to preserve the sensation of continued motion in a position. It is recognisable in the extending gesture which has the feeling and appearance of going on into space, a feeling created by the bodily tension and distant focus of the eyes.

Many expressive and subtle examples of these stillnesses may be studied in sculpture. The standing, seated and reclining figures of Michaelangelo, Rodin and Moore are good examples.

When children stop and hold still with their teacher their class-teacher contact is intensified.

No mention has been made so far, in this chapter, of walking, for this form of locomotion is extremely difficult to do expressively in a dance context. It requires great control and strong powers of concentration. However, classes which have already experienced exploration in travelling and stepping will develop still further through tasks requiring variations in walking. These tasks may be concerned with the placing of the body weight over the point of support. In one variation the weight might be forward over the toes. This type of walk will be appropriate when eagerness to reach a destination is important and it can have a strong, positive expression. If the body leans forward too much then the strength is lost and is replaced by a weak expression close to toppling over. The last expression may take on a comic and playful character when the teacher creates a happy mood.

In a second variation, the weight may be more backward over the heels. This creates a sense of holding back or reluctance to progress. It has the conflicting feeling of actually going forwards while retreating in intention. It may become fearful in expression or, when exaggerated, comic.

Further exploration would bring about variations in which the placing of the weight was more on one side of the body than the other, creating an uneven kind of walk which might become lilting, or more grotesque, as in limping movements.

From an exploration of the material presented in this chapter a repertoire of dance movements could be built. This repertoire would enable the children to make effective use of the subject matter for the dances considered in Chapter 4.

SUMMARY

1. **Action**

Every dance lesson includes action of the whole body. There are five bodily actions:

   (*a*) Travelling and stepping.
   (*b*) Contracting and extension.
   (*c*) Jumping.
   (*d*) Turning and twisting.
   (*e*) Gesturing.

Through exploration the child is encouraged to discover action variations.

A *Travelling and stepping variations* include:

   (*a*) Big steps and small steps.
   (*b*) Feet together and feet apart.
   (*c*) Feet passing by each other.
   (*d*) One foot approaching the other.
   (*e*) Both feet stopping simultaneously.
   (*f*) Feet stopping one after the other.

B *Turning variations* include:

   (*a*) Turning to focus (various degrees from a quarter to a complete turn).
   (*b*) The sensation of turning is experienced in:
      (i) Spinning with pattering feet.
      (ii) Pivoting on one foot.
      (iii) Whirling.
   (*c*) Head turning followed by the body and vice versa.

C *Jumping variations* include:
   (a) Jumping into the air.
   (b) Jumping off the ground.
   (c) Jumping from two feet to two feet.
   (d) Jumping from one foot to the same foot (hop). Alternating the supporting foot (skipping).
   (e) Jumping from one foot to two feet.
   (f) Jumping from two feet to one foot.
   (g) Jumping from one foot to the other foot.
   (h) Jumping with focus upward or downward.

D *Contracting and extending variations* include:
   (a) Whole body contracting or extending.
   (b) One part starting and others following.
   (c) The right side contracting or extending more than the left (asymmetric).
   (d) The left and right sides contracting or extending equally (symmetric).

E *Gesturing variations* include:
   (a) Hands gesturing.
      (i) Gripping and extending.
     (ii) Palms smoothing, pressing, lifting, facing each other, turning away from each other.
    (iii) Edges of the hands leading, slicing, or cutting gestures.
     (iv) Fists pounding.
      (v) Hand extension led by the finger tips.
     (vi) Hands slapping each other or the floor.
    (vii) Hands slapping the knees.
   (b) Arm gesture.
      (i) Tracing pathways in the air.
     (ii) Extending and contracting.
    (iii) Gathering and scattering.

These variations on bodily action are the obvious ones. Children will extend their vocabulary of movement through experiencing them. In action, the stress may be put on the whole body activity or on the action of a particular part of the body, such as hands, elbows or knees.

2. Body Awareness

Body awareness develops through the experience of activities emphasising particular parts of the body. In dance education action activities develop the child's awareness of the parts of his body.

At first the child becomes aware of his whole body in action; then

c

the extremities; the elbows and knees and finally the body centre, hips and chest.

3. The ability to be still without losing the expressive character of the movement is an important part of body awareness.

FURTHER READING

Laban (16): Chapters 2 and 3 contain clear descriptions of variations on the bodily actions.

North (23): In chapter 2 there are examples of action sequences in phrases.

Russell: (32 and 33): Both of these books give help on teaching bodily actions.

Preston-Dunlop (26): See the chapter on Theme vi for further study of the actions of the body.

II DYNAMIC ACTION

Through dance the child experiences movement expressive of not only the emotions but moods, more diffuse states. These expressions are revealed mainly by the movement dynamics. In the dance situation the child is in control of these moods, while in real life the moods often take control of the child. It is one of the aims in dance education that with the growth of control over movement dynamics, which in real life are the outer expression of an inner state, the child may gain an insight into his real-life moods on the one hand and a sensitivity to the moods of those with whom he comes into contact on the other hand.

The impact of dance movements upon the dancer is the result of the action and the dynamics of the action. Laban recognised that movement dynamics comprise four motion factors which he classified as *flow, weight, time,* and *space*. He also came to the conclusion that the dancer's attitude to these motion factors could be either a *fighting* one or an *indulging* one. It is the teacher's job to develop the child's sensibility, through stimulating action which will help the child to experience these motion factors. In the following pages each factor is considered in turn.

1. *The Motion Factor – Flow*

FLOW may be BOUND or FREE. Free flow may be experienced through unrestrained and continuous travelling. The action of stopping is usually achieved by binding flow but it is possible to halt slow travelling steps without binding the flow. In this case the sensation of moving is prolonged even in the stillness. The child's awareness of flow may be developed by tasks involving going continuously, hesitating, pausing and stopping. Leaping, whirling, and travelling with continuous steps and turning jumps are all actions which encourage free flow. Free flow movement often originates in the centre of the body and travels outwards, influencing first the shoulder joint and then the elbow, wrist and hand, or the hip joint and then the knee and foot. Bound flow on the contrary often originates in the extremities and travels inwards as in gestures where the palm pushes out from the body into space. Here the flow starts in the hand and then involves elbow, shoulder and trunk.

The actions of contracting and extending, stepping, and rising and sinking will be helpful in giving children bound flow experience, and the actions of swaying, turning, travelling and leaping will be helpful in giving children free flow experience.

2. *The Motion Factor – Weight*

Strong forceful movement is sometimes referred to as FIRM TOUCH movement. The opposite kind of movement which is characterised by light tension is sometimes referred to as FINE TOUCH movement. Maximum resistance to weight produces strong powerful movement of great tension. Decreasing this resistance to weight will produce delicate light movement till past a certain degree any further decrease in resistance will result in increasing heaviness. Complete relaxation of our resistance to weight, as when we give in to gravity, results in a sinking movement and if the resistance is relaxed abruptly, a collapse. In leaping we have the sensation of overcoming gravity completely for an instant but part of the pleasure in leaping lies in feeling the pull of gravity during the fall prior to landing. Classical ballet aims to defy gravity and to avoid giving in to it as much as possible. In modern ballet and in modern educational dance giving in to gravity is as important as resisting gravity. An imbalance in our movement towards giving in to gravity results in a passivity, and tends to make the mover feel lethargic and floppy. An imbalance the other way results in rigidity.

The play of weight, in accentuating parts of a movement phrase, creates accents at the beginning, middle, or end. When the accent comes at the beginning the movement has an impulsive character because there is no preparation; when it falls in the middle the movement has a swinging character, and when it comes at the end the movement has an impactive character.

Some children have difficulty in experiencing the sensation of heaviness. Swinging type movements will help to give these children a feeling of heaviness as will jumps in which the landing is emphasised. Movement without a feeling for heaviness or weight appears mechanical or inhuman. A good bodily understanding of weight contributes to movement vitality. A soft light quality may be induced by rising actions which result in the heels leaving the ground. Participation with the front of the chest area helps achieve buoyancy in the rising. This movement should be accompanied by a gentle inhalation and has a slight expansive feeling. In this movement the whole body extends with light tension. The extension is in the spine but the whole body should be involved; no part being allowed to hang or droop. Leading with the back of the hand helps when aiming for gestures with a light tension, while clenching the fist and gripping in the elbows, knees and abdomen help the child to produce strong, powerful movement. Pushing and pulling actions are also effective in promoting a sensation of strength. Stamping, pounding with the fists, slapping the knees with the palms of the hands and clapping are all good examples of strong movement. Powerful action may be produced by leading with the elbows in sinking. Strong thrusting leaps, leaps which whip round in the air, and skipping with strong emphasis on the hitting knee action are also helpful actions in aiming for forceful movement.

3. *The Motion Factor – Time*
Real suddenness has a feeling of urgency coupled with a sharp

desire to reach the end of the movement. It is extremely exhausting if continued for long. Real sustainment has a feeling of being caught up in an unending stream of time. The movement is leisurely as the dancer lingers over each stage, unwilling to give it up. A balanced time 'sense' results in an ability to keep abreast of things, neither rushing madly on to the next job nor letting things get so far ahead of one that panic ensues. Contracting gestures where the arms are drawn in towards the body are easy to do suddenly. Children can bring the hands together with suddenness. Little jumps and rapid steps about the spot also help in giving children an experience of suddenness. Sustainment may be felt successfully in contractions and extensions, stepping and gesturing.

4. *The Motion Factor – Space*

An indulgent attitude to space results in a plasticity of bodily action. The movement will either be expansive and fill the space about the body or fold flexibly in the space. It will have a definite relation to the body centre; originating there when it is a whole body movement. The eyes often have an inward-looking focus. A fighting attitude to the space results in an economic use of space in a definite single area about the body. The focus will often be an outer one with clear singleness of purpose and exact aim. It will originate more at the extremities instead of at the body centre. A fighting attitude to space may be experienced in penetrating and cutting gestures and in travelling when the destination is clear and the pathway to it undeviating. An indulgent attitude to space may be experienced in flexibly performed shrinking and expanding movements and in travelling where the pathways wind and the body enters into the pathways in a mobile way.

PROGRESSION IN DYNAMIC CONTROL

When children are moving with particular awareness of one of these four factors it is recognised that the other factors are present as well. For example, when we are concentrating on the time factor the movement still occupies space, and has its own particular weight stress and degree of flow, but time is uppermost in consciousness. When, however, an awareness of each factor is sufficiently developed for a child to show a command of each single factor in his movement, then it is possible for him to begin to be challenged to move with full consciousness of two factors at the same time. Movement which stresses two motion factors simultaneously is recognisable as a definite mode. Through these modes of movement children will find a vehicle for their subjective feelings and moods. In Middle School, children will be making the physical and psychological transitions associated with early adolescence. During this phase of growth, movement exploration and dance composition centred on dynamics offer opportunities for developing an understanding of the dynamic variations expressive of our subjective feelings and moods. Any two of the four motion factors – weight, flow, time and space – may be combined with each other. In this way it is possible to make six combinations: weight/time, weight/flow, weight/space, space/time, space/flow and flow/time. Each pair may be contrasted by an opposite pair. Arranged in opposite pairs we have: weight/time, space/flow, weight/flow, space/time, weight/space, flow/time. Each of these three opposite pairs will be considered in the following pages.

1. (a) *Weight/Time*

Weight/time combinations produce movement of rhythmic vitality or calm gentleness. In stressing suddenness with light tension the movement sparks out and quickly dies. Powerful and sudden dynamics is possible in jumps, gestures and contractions. Dynamic variations in the touch of the feet on the floor or in a hand-to-hand touch are useful in giving children experience in these combinations of weight and time factors. The touch may be firm or gentle, and may come about with suddenness or sustainment.

1. (b) *Space/Flow*

Emphasis on space/flow combinations brings about free flow or bound flow movement which uses space in a flexible or direct way. Turning jumps and expansive twists help to promote generous and indulgent use of space. Careful extensions and guided contractions will promote a restricted use of space. Controlled and aimed movement which pierces space and pliant movement which undulates in space both bring about this mode of movement. Space flow combinations may also be felt by stressing shape and position, the changes from one position to another being unhampered and free in flow or careful, cautious, and bound in flow.

2. (a) Flow/Weight

Phrases of light fluent travelling followed by strong bound flow sinking actions are within the dynamic possibilities of this mode. Strength in the sinking may follow delicacy in the rising. Buoyancy and strength alternating in continuous leaping combines free flow with weight changes. Flow combined with weight may also be experienced in gentle and unrestrained spiralling up from deep positions followed by strong and bound flow sinking. Flow may be released, with strength in deep swinging actions which lead to spinning and turning jumps, and bound by checking the swing or the turning till stillness results. Asymmetric and symmetric expansion and contraction motifs are suitable for variations in flow and weight.

2. (b) Space/Time

The body knotting slowly in space and unravelling suddenly brings about this combination. Sudden steps which are precisely placed may be contrasted with slow weaving pathways which take on a figure eight pattern. Phrases which stress space and time may include aimed movements which pierce the space suddenly or slowly. Darting gestures or sustained movements of hands and feet and stirring movements of the whole body will also give the experience of space/time combinations.

3. (a) Weight/Space

Movement in this mode includes strong twisting and gentle untwisting. Sharp pointed gestures leading the whole body into strong extensions may precede strong pulling movements bringing the limbs back home to the body centre. Elbows can initiate strong gestures which follow straight pathways in the air or merely extend outwards from the body centre and then return to it again. Undulating and rotating movements may start in the hand and involve the whole body eventually with strength or gentleness. Wrestling movements whilst gripping hands with a partner, either both hands or one, will promote flexibility and strength. A pair sequence might begin with strong gripping and end with more delicate touch, where one leads the other directly, or in a more flexible way, through the space.

3. (b) *Time/Flow*

Free flow combined with suddenness may be experienced in movement consisting of small sudden jumps separated by rapid preparatory steps. Medium-sized extensions and contractions facilitate experience of sustainment and bound flow. In swaying, leading to turning which speeds up and slows down to a stop, the flow may free in the turn and bind in the stopping. Stops and starts which occur gradually or suddenly help to bring about the time/flow experience.

It will be clear from the above descriptions that the teacher's choice of words is important in stimulating these dynamic variations. Words like crushing or squeezing encourage strength, whereas smoothing and cutting draw attention to space. Frequently words imply more than one quality. Words like this are therefore useful in promoting movement consisting of combinations of two motion factors. For example 'pounce' and 'yawn' draw attention to time and space; 'sinuous' and 'pushing' to weight and space; 'swinging' to flow and weight and 'stalking' to flow and time.

There are six modes of movement considered above and within each mode there are four dynamic variations. In the mode of movement stressing weight/time, for instance, there is forcefulness with suddenness; forcefulness with sustainment, light tension with suddenness and light tension with sustainment. This gives twenty-four dynamic variations which may with some experience be distinguished. The richness which this dynamic range brings to the child's dance vocabulary is clearly considerable.

The teacher may notice that certain children prefer particular modes. Such preferences are a part of each child's movement character. The fact that some fight time or indulge in time was mentioned earlier in this chapter. Personality traits are revealed by our demonstration of a preference for the fighting attitude or the indulging attitude. Children who show a bent towards suddenness and forcefulness are fighters of both the motion's factors. It is neither good nor bad that we are fighters or indulgers in this sense. A community has a place for all types of personalities. But is *is* a bad thing if an exaggerated fighting attitude or an exaggerated indulging attitude is demonstrated. The teacher will be able to recognise such an imbalance in a child and will be able to counteract this tendency towards one dynamic factor or mode by giving that child experiences of an opposite dynamic kind. Within the same dynamic range, subtle shades of expression are inevitable. Two children moving with forceful suddenness may differ from each other in the degree of either suddenness or force, which they use. It is partly subtleties of this kind which make each dancer unique. The teacher must try to recognise each child's dynamic potential and foster its development towards maturity.

SUMMARY

1. The teacher aims to provide opportunities for the child to develop an understanding of movement dynamics through dance experiences in which bodily action, mental action, and inner feeling influence each other in a reciprocal way.

2. The child's understanding of movement dynamics progresses through the following stages of their ability to move with:

(*a*) free flow
    bound flow
    fine touch
    firm touch
    sustainment
    suddenness
    flexibility
    directness

(b) (i) firm touch together with suddenness
firm touch together with sustainment
fine touch together with suddenness
fine touch together with sustainment

(ii) flexibility together with free flow
flexibility together with bound flow
directness together with free flow
directness together with bound flow

(iii) free flow together with firm touch
free flow together with fine touch
bound flow together with firm touch
bound flow together with fine touch

(iv) flexibility together with sustainment
flexibility together with suddenness
directness together with sustainment
directness together with suddenness

(v) firm touch together with flexibility
firm touch together with directness
fine touch together with flexibility
fine touch together with directness

(vi) suddenness together with free flow
suddenness together with bound flow
sustainment together with free flow
sustainment together with bound flow.

FURTHER READING

North (23): Chapter 3 will lead the reader to an appreciation of the principles of movement governing movement dynamics.

Russell (34): The chapter 'Effort' is important reading for a fuller understanding of this aspect of movement.

Preston-Dunlop (26): Chapters 2 and 4 describe the four motion factors in detail.

North (37): This book is suitable for advanced study of effort.

III   ACTION IN SPACE

When we consider the infinite number of ways in which action may occupy the space a variety of movement images spring to mind. Some movement takes hold of the space and confines it within the span of the gestures; some movement swerves or swoops through the space; some movement steals into the space gliding sidewards to enter and exit while leaving behind a web of delicate traces; and some movement shrinks from the space to settle at the tangible level of the floor.

During this kind of action the child orientates by relating his movements to reference points in space. These reference points are:

1. The body centre
2. The floor
3. The other parts of the body
4. A partner.

The floor and the body centre are fixed reference points; the other parts of the body may move but are predictable, and a partner is often unpredictable as a reference point.

1. *Relating Movement to the Body Centre*

In considering this reference point the actions of contracting and extending are important. In these actions gesture can extend from the body centre and return again to it like rays. The eye focus is normally outwards when the body extends and inwards when the body contracts. The extension may be linear, plane-like or three-dimensional. In a linear extension the gesture may lead the whole body upwards into a tall narrow position; in a plane-like extension the arms may spread like an horizon, giving an impression of breadth, while one foot moves sidewards into a wide stance; and in a three-dimensional extension each limb may take up a different area of space in either a spoke-like or a pliant way, bringing the body into positions characterised either by their angularity or roundness. The contraction is usually accompanied by a sinking down towards the floor which results in a concertina-like position. It is easier to appreciate the expansive and free nature of the extension after holding the contraction for a moment.

Quite a different expression is felt if the gesture of the limbs relates to the body centre by sweeping around it in a circular or elliptical manner. Here the body will be led into twisting, dipping and leaning. In the early stages in dance the attention should be firmly placed on the bodily feeling rather than the aerial pathway. A curving gesture may swing the body into an open and broad position or as is the case when the gesture curves across the front of the body, a narrow position.

2. *Relating Movement to the Floor*

The spot the child dances in may be taken as a territory from which he travels and to which he returns. He can dance within this spot, his territory, or dance around it with feet keeping close to the floor and making definite contact, or leap out of this spot so that he rises above it for a moment ready to land back down into it. He may leap away from one spot to another spot while keeping his focus on the original and then leap or rush back to the original again. The horizontal nature of the floor may be emphasized by smooth level travelling without rise of fall or by sliding gestures where the sole of the foot keeps in touch with the floor. In the former the relationship of the whole body to the floor is stressed and in the latter the relationship of the foot only to the floor.

The hands too may dance in relationship to the floor, varying from touching or being near, to being far from the floor. The palms of the hands can sense the smoothness and horizontal nature of the floor in sliding or smoothing gestures and keep a constant distance from the floor in swaying movements which lead to turns.

Other parts of the body may come into play in relating to the floor. For example one knee, or one elbow or both elbows, may be stressed in movements approaching the floor. The resulting movement will bring the whole body into deep, crouching, kneeling or sitting positions. In contrast, using the same joints in drawing up away from the floor will bring about angular positions which may have varied character. Some may hover in suspension at their height balanced on one foot with eyes fixed on the floor; some may rear up powerfully by pushing the feet against the floor, some may rise with utmost smoothness, changing imperceptibly from a rooted position near the floor to an elevated position which gives the impression of weightlessness, and others may spring out of the floor to hang for a moment in the air before dropping back to the floor.

At this point it is worth remembering that for the child the end position of a movement is often more readily remembered than the movement itself. For example, it is an easier task for the child to experience what a deep crouching position feels like than to appreciate the process of sinking. Similarly, it is easier to experience what it feels like to be stretched and high on the toes than to appreciate the process of rising. Commands such as 'Stop high up', or 'Stop low down' are helpful in encouraging beginners to attend to spatial situations. Part of the bodily feeling associated with rising and sinking is due to the degree of resistance to gravity.

3. *Relating Movements to the Parts of the Body*

Stopping at the end of a travelling phrase so that the feet are close together and touching, or far apart, focuses attention on placing in the space. In these instances the feet are reference points for each other. Short steps where the feet are close together, followed by long steps where the feet go far apart, contrast the restricted bodily feeling of the former with the freer feeling of the latter. The increase in the size of the steps should be echoed in the extension of the accompanying arm gestures. Close quick steps bring the arms near to the body whereas big steps promote gestures where the arms move further out from the body.

Many possibilities exist in activity where the elbows contrast, being near to or touching the knees and being far from the knees.

The hands may explore this same theme of 'near and far'. They can be near each other and far from each other. Descriptions of dancing based on this activity may be read in Chapter 2 (pp. 28 and 29).

4. *Relating Movement to a Partner*

Spatial awareness is more demanding in this instance because the partner or the group may also be on the move. The child may gradually build confidence for improvising on 'near and far' with a partner, through tasks such as 'Stop near to another person', 'Stop facing your partner', 'Stop side by side with your partner', 'Follow in your partner's pathway', and 'Surround your partner'. Upon simple beginnings like this more subtle dance sequences may be built at a later stage in which the words and phrases, above, below, around, through, underneath, making a roof, mirroring, and shadowing would be relevant. Descriptions of movement stimulated by these words will be found in Chapter 5.

EXPLORATION OF THE SPACE AROUND THE BODY

Once the child's dance shows an awareness of the spatial reference points he may be taught to make use of the areas above, below, at the side of, in front of, and behind. Gestures of the arms may dip into these areas, with various dynamic stresses. For instance, the fists can whip into the air above the head in clenching, or glide smoothly down to the floor level in releasing. The two areas above and below are used in these examples but any two areas might be used. Laban called these areas 'zones'. He discusses these zones in *Choreutics* (15). At first it is easier for the *arms* to gesture into, out of or through these zones. But further progress is made when the legs can also gesture fluently. Progress in using spatial areas depends on learning the bodily feeling associated with movement in each area. For instance, the trunk adjustments made in gesturing in the area behind are part of the bodily feeling associated with this movement, and in gesturing at the side, the trunk rotation is important.

In Spanish dance the castanets play above the head, behind the body and at the side while chittering and clacking their rhythmic accompaniment. In these dances subtle variations in the transitions from one area to another are characterised by little arabesques and rotations of hand and wrist.

The teacher must ensure that the whole body participates in these movement explorations. Any change in the position of the arms should affect not only the immediate body parts, such as the shoulders, but the trunk, head, legs and feet, unless it is the intention to gesture with the arms only. In gesturing near to the body the gesturing limbs will usually be contracted and in gesturing far from the body centre, extended. In harmonious action an extending gesture should have a sympathetic extension in the whole body and a contracting gesture a sympathetic contraction. If an extending arm gesture is accompanied by a contracting movement in the body then a more dramatic expression results. These oppositions in the body are typical of Spanish dance and Indian classical dance. After work on tasks emphasising a *single* area children may at a later stage then compose phrases in which *more than one* area is used. In these phrases they could also vary the dynamics. For example the gesture might plunge downwards into the area near the floor, and then cautiously glide through the area at the right side of the body to finally pause above the head. The accompanying action may vary too. The plunge downwards may happen with a closing turn, the glide to the side with an opening turn and the final gesture upwards with an extension of the whole body. Further exploration might incorporate the gesture variations discussed in Section I of this chapter.

MOVEMENT SCALE

The scale of movement may be grand or miniature. When the movement scale is clearly established the resulting dance takes on a definite character. We associate certain kinds of dance with a particular scale. One would expect a heroic dance for example to be on the grand scale; with sweep and breadth of gesture which amply fills the space. If on the contrary the gesture was cut short, then the grandeur of scale would be diminished.

The word 'scale' implies more than mere 'size' but for the child who is beginning dance 'size' will be a better choice of word in the exploration of this theme, and the contrast between a small action and a big action will constitute a suitable activity. In choosing suitable action the teacher might select jumping, contracting and extending, gesture, or stepping. The child may then make big jumps and small jumps, full and half contractions, big and small gestures, and big and small steps.

When children show good control of the size of action then the teacher may aim to teach the class more about scale in its fuller sense. If the movement sweeps from one part of the room to another with generous extensions and breadth of gesture then an expansiveness is given to the movement. If, on the contrary, it remains more confined to the spot and the gesture occurs near the body which shrinks slightly, then the movement takes on a miniature-like scale. An example of the former would be a running pathway followed by a turning leap. An example of the latter would be a contraction with a turn, followed by a rising arm gesture while the rest of the body remains in the contraction. The task 'show me by your movement that you have only a small space to move in', often helps the child to reduce his movement to the minimum size. A contrasting task might be 'Now explode out of this small space and see how much space you can fill with your movement'.

In connection with the theme of movement scale it is revealing to study the sculpture of Henry Moore. Even his small reclining sculptures only a few inches long have a monumental look about them. Henry Moore himself confesses an inability to explain what it is that makes for monumentality. He suggests that it might have something to do with the subordination of the details to the essentials. This ability to keep a sense of the whole while giving a finish to the details is an advanced achievement in dance. If an opening gesture has a little ornamental deviation on the way which does not detract from the breadth of the gesture then this would be a very simple example in dance of keeping a sense of the whole while making a detail clear.

STILLNESS AND SHAPE

In this chapter the development of a spatial sense is now seen to have three stages; the relating of movement to a reference point; the locating of movement in areas about the body and the varying of the movement scale. While the child is improving his understanding in these aspects he may sharpen his sense of position or shape by attending to stillness. Stillness gives the child an opportunity to feel the relationship between the parts of the body. It is not advisable however to stress 'making a shape' because this encourages meaningless posing. When stillness is the result of a movement being stopped the position will then be expressive and not contrived or artificial. Commands like 'go' and 'stop' are sufficient to produce meaningful stillnesses *if* the child has an action vocabulary. The choice of action may be left to the child. When the class stops and holds the position the teacher, by asking appropriate questions, will focus the child's attention on the shape. He might ask for example: 'Are your feet together or apart?', 'Are you spread out or narrow?', 'Are you twisted?', 'Are you contracted or extended?', 'Are you high or low?'. The teacher will know from observing the finishing positions around him at that moment in the hall what particular questions to ask. He can also say 'Look at John's position and notice how near the ground he is', or 'Do you seee how flat a shape Jack's position makes?'. The 'feeling' for shape in dance is awakening particularly at the eight and nine-year-old stage. Control of shape in dance and the opportunity to observe shape changes is part of the aesthetic pleasure fostered in movement education. The words of the sculptor Kenneth Armitage, quoted by Carola Giedion-Welcker in her book *Contemporary Sculpture* (6, p. 210), show a particular preoccupation with shape in the following quotation. He writes:

The discovery of flatness has dominated my work for the time being. . . . Pleasure from wondering what is on the other side. Pleasure from the division. Pleasure from seeing washing hanging on a line.

At this point it is noteworthy that awareness of shape is not confined to the visual appreciation, or a bodily sensation of length, compactness or breadth, but tactile appreciation as well. This underlines the value to the child of appreciating the flatness of the floor by contact with it, the flatness of the palm by contact with his partner's palm or the contact of his own palms meeting each other. Henry Moore (11, p. 131) in talking of his sculptures writes:

Whenever I see this figure I am reminded of a boyhood experience that contributed towards the conception of its form. I was a Yorkshire miner's son, the youngest of seven and my mother was no longer so very young. She suffered from bad rheumatism in the back and would often say to me in Winter when I came back from school, 'Henry, boy, come and rub my back'. Then I would massage her back with liniment. When I came to this figure (a seated sculpture) which represents a fully mature woman, I found that I was unconsciously giving to its back the long forgotten shape of the one I had so often rubbed as a boy. . . .

Among the positions resulting from arresting the flow of

D

movement some may have a look and feeling of stability while others have an exciting feeling of instability and asymmetry. This phenomenon leads us to a consideration of equilibrium.

EQUILIBRIUM

In dance, equilibrium is concerned with repose and lack of repose. In dance education the words stability and lability are used. Stability refers to balancing or anchoring in movement, and is character-ised by positions and movements which are four-square and broad-based. Stable stances are rooted in the floor. Lability refers to being out of balance and is characterised by movements which lean and tilt. Labile stances are impossible since balance is neces-sary in order to have a stance. A form of lability may be ex-perienced by leaning out of balance until steps have to be taken to prevent a fall, or by making jumps and turns which lean and tilt in the air. In the tilting the body may be straight or curved. A semi-labile sensation is experienced when the hip region is pushed out of the body's plumb line during turns, steps, or rising and sinking.

In the initial stages the child may be given an experience of these two conditions by movement activity stressing symmetry and asymmetry. Asymmetry is exciting and leads to movement. Symmetry is restful and inhibits movement. Jumping, rising, sinking, turning, spreading, closing, contracting and extending may all be performed symmetrically or asymmetrically.

Sculptors are very conscious of equilibrium. The sculptor Maillol (6, p. 26) recognised the asymmetry of much of Rodin's work and reacted with the following words:

I felt I must return to more stable and self-contained forms.

Stability and lability are important factors in the ordering and harmonising of forms in space. Carola Giedion-Welcker (6, p. 216) describes Walter Bodmer's work:

The wire compositions of Walter Bodmer, the Swiss sculptor and painter, unfold in space, delicate and fantastic as spiders' webs. Rising and falling movement and swaying flight are expressed in many variations and rhythms ... the quivering balance of these subtle constructions seems to ignore the law of gravity.

It is a healthy dance education which gives the child opportunities to experience labile movement as well as stable movement. If a child's movement shows an exaggerated one sidedness towards either of these types of equilibrium then he should be given movement tasks which promote the contrary kind of equilibrium.

PATHWAYS IN SPACE

Satisfaction and enjoyment from movement concerned with spatial pathways depends on background experience in the earlier themes considered in this chapter.

There are three kinds of spatial pathways:

(*a*) Straight one-dimensional paths.
(*b*) Curved two-dimensional paths.
(*c*) Winding three-dimensional paths.

Straight one-dimensional paths

As straight pathways are not the most natural pathways for the body to trace, the joints and trunk have to co-ordinate in order to achieve this action. The resulting movement acquires a certain intensity because of its singleness of focus and undeviating nature.

Pathways of this kind may be achieved by jumps, travelling, extensions and contractions in which the movements radiate outwards from the body centre and inwards towards the body centre, and by gestures of the limbs.

Curved two-dimensional paths

Two-dimensional movement occurs frequently in everyday behaviour. It is characterised by gradual change of direction which gives to the movement a lyrical character.

Curved pathways may be made by gesturing, gesturing and turning, and gesturing and travelling. The pattern of a curved pathway may be clarified by having a regard for the centre which the curving pathway surrounds. Opportunities to practise movement which describes curved pathways will bring greater fluidity to the child's dance.

Winding three-dimensional paths

These pathways knot and unwind in the space. They make patterns resembling an S shape which has been twisted, and demand bodily plasticity in their performance.

Turning jumps, rotating gestures, and spiralling movements which change half-way up or down from clockwise to anti-clockwise turning will help to make these pathways.

Paul Klee and Jean Arp in their drawings reveal sensitivity and ingenuity in composing pathways. Their drawings show the surprisingly varied expressions which may emerge from exploring this theme.

It is now obvious that the expressive impact of movement owes as much to spatial orientation as dynamic character. In the following quotation Beryl de Zoete (4, p. 223) brings part of a Balinese dance to life by her magical description. She writes:

The dancers have resumed an excited, sharply accentuated dance, with wide and swift-circling movements. So far as they represent any one, they are now the King of Lasem and his attendant. After a brief pause they rise and dance side by side in vast animation. Everything, from their flowery crowns to their fluttering feet, is accent and glittering precision. Their fans twist and whirr like fishes' fins. Face to face, back to back, dipping, curving, shuffling, now poised on one leg, now on the other, continually sinking to the ground and rising in an endless undulation, with infinite indirections of their progress. The line of their movement blossoms, like Balinese drawings, into smaller intricacies of circular pattern, knotted by accents of eye, neck, or finger, hip or knee or toes so that a single dancer seems to carry within her small body a whole orchestra of movement. Even in this very vivid passage a movement seldom sets in suddenly. It has its own delicate anacrusis, it gets under way: and this gives a peculiar feeling of elasticity. Each curve, however swiftly performed, is arrested by a break so subtle that one is only conscious of it as the rebound of a bough that has been drawn down and flies back again when freed.

Here, orientation and dynamic change are imperceptibly interwoven.

SUMMARY

There are seven themes in this chapter considered in order of difficulty. It is not intended that one should be mastered before going on to the next. Overlapping may often occur.

The Themes

1. Tasks in which the child relates his movements to reference points help to develop his ability to orientate. There are four reference points:

    (*a*) The body-centre
    (*b*) The floor
    (*c*) The other parts of the body
    (*d*) A partner.

2. Location
    Movement clarity depends on placing the movement accurately in six principal areas:

    (*a*) Above
    (*b*) Below
    (*c*) In front
    (*d*) Behind
    (*e*) At the side

    Learning in this theme depends not only on clear placing but on building a vocabulary of bodily feelings associated with movements in each of these areas.

3. Movement Scale
    The scale of movement relates to two factors:

    (*a*) The degree of extension or contraction
    (*b*) The amount of space occupied.

4. Stillness
    In stillness the child has time to feel the relationship between the parts of his body and to become aware of body shape.

5. Equilibrium
    Balance in movement is related to co-ordination and poise. Understanding of this theme develops through the play between two states.

    (*a*) Stability
    (*b*) Lability.

6. Pathways
    There are three kinds of pathway:

    (*a*) Straight one-dimensional pathways
    (*b*) Curved two-dimensional pathways
    (*c*) Winding three-dimensional pathways.

FURTHER READING

North (23): Chapter 4 and Chapter 7 describe how this aspect of movement may be used to stimulate creative work.

Russell (34): The chapter 'Space' is important reading for a fuller understanding of this aspect of movement.

Preston-Dunlop (26): An introduction to the theme of 'Space' will be found in Chapter 3.

IV   IN ACTION TOGETHER

> And hand in hand, on the edge of the sand,
> They danced by the light of the Moon, . . .
>
> Edward Lear, 'The Owl and the Pussycat'

In what ways does dancing alone differ from dancing with others? In the first situation the child is concerned with himself or the surroundings, while in the second he is concerned with his partners who become an important new focus. This new focus both draws the child's attention outwards and becomes an exciting part of the surroundings. As in everyday living the ability to preoccupy oneself as an individual is as important as the ability to share preoccupations with others, so every dance lesson should offer the child opportunities for both of these experiences. Sections I, II and III of this chapter have considered the material content of the dance lesson and how the material might be explored by the individual. This section will consider wherever appropriate how the same material may be explored in a group situation.

BASIC RELATIONSHIP EXPERIENCES

Class/teacher relationships

Numerous variations in travelling and moving on the spot may be shared with a leader. The teacher makes a good leader in the early stages.

All age groups will enjoy movement experiences which are shared as a class with the teacher. The teacher may be the focus for travelling phrases in which the class approaches, arriving by the teacher, and withdraws, arriving in a spot at some distance from the teacher. The class will appreciate the proximity on arriving near the teacher and the separateness after withdrawing If the teacher shifts her position in the room the children will find themselves in new places in the group which forms during the advancing. In advancing and retreating motifs the action may be varied. The advancing could be managed by travelling or jumping; the withdrawal by turning as well as travelling. The arrival might be stressed by asking the class to arrive with a jump. The relationship will be reinforced by encouraging stillness on arrival and at the end of the withdrawal. If the teacher can give a cue either vocally or instrumentally for stopping, this will help the class not only to stop together but to note the group rhythm.

To explore the dynamic possibilities within this situation one can vary the quality of the movement. The class might for instance advance with stamping steps or quiet fine touch steps, advance with a rush and withdraw in sustainment; or advance with control and caution as in bound flow and withdraw with abandoned turning and jumping as in free flow.

When the class is gathered near the teacher, group actions of rising, sinking and swaying may occur. In the rising and sinking the gesture of hands may become important; in the swaying the flow.

These shared situations will often help establish concentration at the beginning of lessons and then lead into more individual work. At the end of lessons they will often give a sense of climax and help establish a calmness before the class leaves to go to another teacher.

Pair relationships

After situations in which the class advances towards the teacher, the tasks might be set for each individual to advance towards his partner. Thus the motif employed within the class/teacher relationship now serves the pair. When the partners meet, the actions of jumping, stepping, sinking, and rising would be suitable actions for the partners to do at the same time. In this way short on-the-spot dances may arise. If the pair dance emphasised the dynamics of the action then sudden controlled stamping might begin the dance and sustained fine touch stepping conclude it. On the other hand a spatial stress might demand meeting with long striding steps and moving together on the spot with small steps.

Partner dances will often include travelling and stopping. Travelling around a partner may be complete or partial. Focusing on a partner while surrounding him results in rotations of the head and chest region bringing the pair into more twisted shapes which interlock the partners. Definite relationships can be established between partners by completely circling or facing each other. A less definite character is given to relationships when partners are side on or when one circles the other who revolves on the spot. Children should enjoy opportunities for experiencing all of these situations. The self-contained nature of the territory between two partners is emphasised when they link by touching palms or by grasping each other's wrists or elbows. The proximity and resulting intimacy is enjoyed by children. The stylisation of historic dances at Court veiled this intimacy and in our English and Irish folk dances it is formalised by strict geometric pattern and rules.

In on the spot dances in pairs, jumps, low and kept near the floor, from two feet to two feet would contrast with high light jumps which get up off the floor into the air. If the partners vary dancing together with taking turns, then one partner might do a deep bouncing, swaying, crouching dance which is answered by the other partners stamping leaping dance. At first the same action should constitute the basis of dances in which the partners take turns but later each partner might dance with his own individual action as in the above example. In the jumping and stepping dances described above there is ample opportunity for stressing feet and knees in the stepping and jumping or elbows and hands. Rising and sinking class/teacher motifs are a good lead-in to duos concerned with rising and sinking. The material in Section I for elbow and knee dances has been found useful for duo motifs. Very simple phrases of travelling and stopping would be suitable for pair dances based on the relationship theme of 'follow your leader'.

Group experiences
Individuals may draw together calmly to form a group by travelling, stepping or jumping and separate explosively or smoothly with jumping, stepping or turning. Words like creeping, stalking, drifting, or rushing are useful in stimulating these activities. Children with dance experience can meet and part with action combinations such as turning jumps, travelling and sinking, or stepping while turning. The bigger the group the more space its meeting territory will occupy. It should be noted whether the groups meet and fill up their territory in bunched together groups with some on the inside and some around the edges (Fig. 1a), or

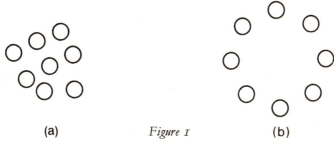

(a) *Figure 1* (b)

stop at a distance from the centre leaving a space which they surround or contain (Fig. 1b). Both of these gatherings should be experienced often enough for them to be absorbed into the child's movement memory. Leaving a space is the more formal formation.

Transient relationship experiences
All of the relationships described above are definite and conscious but there are class situations in which fleeting relationships occur, none the less expressive because of their transience. Such transient relationships exist when the children are travelling in and out of each other, weaving and winding their way in the spaces. The teacher can draw the attention of the class to these movements and exploit them. Each child will often, in this travelling, pass others by, go between, veer and dodge. The teacher, in an effort to stimulate the child's awareness of these movements, may say,

'Let me see clearly by your action how you dodge'. Movement imagination and ingenuity together with the sense of rhythm, dynamics and spatial pattern may be stimulated through this movement activity. Each child should be encouraged when his way of dodging shows clearly any of these aspects of movement. Observation will reveal limitless variety. Some swerve with beautiful body tilts, others dip to the side with bird-like agility, almost brushing the floor while the opposite urge takes some up into labile leaps. Veering to dodge others will frequently bring about turns which lead into winding pathways. The eyes need continual alertness and the whole body a lively readiness to adapt to the changing environment of the movement of others. Dodging activity demands not only readiness to adapt but ability to bring the movement to a halt, to a hesitation, or to a split second stillness; these bindings in flow can be very expressive.

INTERMEDIATE RELATIONSHIP EXPERIENCES

If children have a background of the experiences considered so far, then they will be ready to work more sensitively in twos, threes, and small groups of about seven.

In travelling to meet a partner the task may require the child to show whether he stops facing or sideways on to his partner. Facing is the most intense encounter. A side on placing offers an escape route. The character of these encounters may be emphasised by keeping the placing while going into action together. This might mean jumping facing a partner who shares the same spot with you or stepping sidewards together, swaying together, rising or sinking together. Partners, side by side, can rise and sink, sway, circle, and travel together while maintaining their side to side placing. Travelling towards a partner results in contact, figuratively speaking. In language we have the phrase 'meeting a person half-way'. The four situations in Fig 2 show this situation and three others, the amount of activity of A and B being different in (b), (c) and (d).

When partners meet they are able to confront each other whereas when three persons meet they cannot confront each other but merely converge on a common territory. Pair dances based

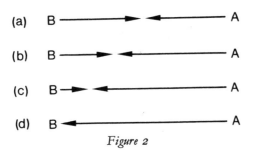

Figure 2

on jumping may consist of jumping together on the spot. Holding hands forces the partners into a common rhythm. Curt Sachs writing about Choral Dances in his *World History of the Dance* says:

In a higher level the Choral dancers almost always touch one another and thus force themselves into the same stride and movement.

Jumping together on the spot can lead to jumping apart and coming together again. While jumping and joining hands the partners may reach a new spot by their action or make their jumps take them around their spot. Holding only one hand allows greater freedom for travelling and thus introduces more mobility. It is worth remembering that unless the dancers hold hands or are united in a common rhythm, jumping tends to loosen the contact or link between the members. On the other hand it is also true that when a close contact or rhythmic link does exist, jumping brings an excitement and vitality to the relationship.

In dance and in everyday life, we turn towards someone to make contact and turn away to break contact. Turning towards brings communication, turning away breaks it. With a partner the turn to each other will alter its expression as the quality alters. It may have a lyric stress, a comic playful stress or a dynamic stress. One may turn to break contact with a partner or turn to enjoy coming back to face a partner for a second time. In spinning around together partners share the dizzy feeling associated with the turning. A may spin B who then spins A.

Turning towards a focus may unite any number of group members. The groups may turn towards a common focus which may be a place in the room, an individual or another group. The focus may be within the group or outside it.

Contracting and extending with a partner or partners brings about varied relationships. Basically, extending together brings partners into each other's view and contracting together results in them withdrawing from each other. When coming into each other's view in extending the eye, contact may be accompanied by hands, or elbows meeting and touching. By varying the time relationship the partners can reach the meeting point after each other or start the extension after each other. The teacher who has the possibilities outlined in Section II in mind will be quick to spot further variations discovered by the child. Bigger groups may contract in approaching a common centre and expand by retreating from it. Although each member of the group uses a common action he may execute his approach and retreat in his own way. Thus, when each individual varies his timing in approaching and retreating, secondary relationships will emerge within the larger unit. In Fig. 3, A, B and C are united in their distance from the centre during their approach. D, E and F are also united in their distance from the centre during their retreat.

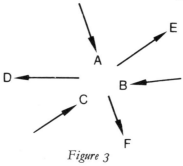

Figure 3

Variations in stepping may constitute the movement content of dances concerned with pairs or group interplay. The following are stepping ideas suitable for pair sequences or sequences concerned with group interplay. A stamping phrase may have a response in which the feet patter or tap. This little conversational fragment might lead to a concluding action in which both parties have a stamping or pattering phrase which they do together. In another sequence one group which uses sliding steps might move at a lower level to a group which answers this sliding step pattern with high pattering steps. Finally, a stamping group could emphasise the static character of their motif which their opposite group responds to with striding steps which are more mobile.

Travelling through the space between two other partners is a situation particularly belonging to the trio. In this situation the partner going through will sense his individuality in contrast to the togetherness of the pair he approaches. Several events may arise from this grouping. The pair may block the individual as he approaches their shared territory, or capture him inside the circle made by their linked arms, join him to form a line, or let him pass through and then follow after him in file thus making him the leader. The three situations illustrated in Fig. 4 are experienced by the partner going between as (*a*) filling a space, (*b*) joining a line, and lastly opposing a pair.

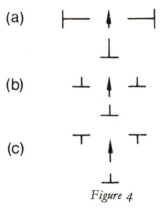

Figure 4

If the two flanking the space were linked the third person might then split the pair as he entered the space between. When three partners travel around a common centre they contain the space within their shared territory more successfully than is possible for only two partners.

In the relationships considered so far the partners and groups have either moved together with the same action or taken turns *using the same action*. Upon a foundation of such experiences more interesting relationship sequences may be composed, from exploratory and improvised beginnings, in which the actions, dynamics and spatial forms of one partner may stimulate quite contrasting reactions from one another partner.

In the earlier work where the partners did the same action variety came within the action from the part of the body stressed, the rhythm, the size of the action and the placing of it in relation to the partner. Now an even greater richness may be encouraged when the action varies also.

ADVANCED RELATIONSHIP EXPERIENCES

From lesson introductions where the teacher gives the class opportunity to work on two actions, lesson development may arise in which one child uses the first action and his partner reacts with the second. For example after an exploratory experience with jumping and travelling, partner A may begin a short composition with a jumping phrase which is answered by a travelling phrase from partner B. In this case since the given material was jumping and travelling the class might be left to choose the dynamics from weight and time factors. Thus A's jumping phrase may comprise strong forceful thrusting jumps and B's travelling may contrast this with calm fine touch. Other actions which might be introduced in pairs as a basis for interaction compositions are turning and travelling, jumping and turning, gesturing and travelling, rising and sinking and travelling, spreading and closing and travelling, and stepping and jumping. To end such compositions both partners could use the same action. The partner whose action is chosen to finish with will tend to appear as the dominant one. For example, if A is a 'jumper' and B is a 'turner' and they end their composition with jumping, then A's jumping has been more influential than B's turning. In this kind of development it would be a further challenge for the partners to aim to show the gradual growth of importance of the jumping phrase up to the moment when the turning disappears. This growth might be demonstrated by A's jumping phrase becoming longer with each repeat, while B's turning phrase gets shorter in duration. The whole dance might then have the following shape: A jump, jump, B turn, turn, A jump, jump, jump, B turn, A and B jump, jump, jump, jump.

If the introduction to a lesson gave opportunities for the class to experience free flow and bound flow in different actions, then a composition task might ask for a dance in which A's free flow was answered by B's bound flow. The class could be asked to show whether A and B finish with the same element of flow, or whether A and B exchange their qualities, or whether they stick to their own uncompromisingly. After the introduction in which everybody experienced the actions used to introduce the flow experiences, the class could be left to choose which of the actions they preferred for their sequence.

A similar compositional structure might be used with an introduction which has a spatial theme instead of an action theme, or a dynamic one. In these compositions involving interaction in twos or threes, the teacher must look for and encourage reactions which are appropriate. For example, if A's jump brings A into a finishing position in front of B, then B may begin his turning reaction by turning away from A. Again if A's spreading action finishes with his right hand ending above B's head, B's travelling reaction may bring B to a position below A's left hand. Lastly, if A's gestures towards B are all led with the elbows, then B's withdrawing turns may all be led with the same joint. In this way B is always showing an awareness of A's movement.

At first in inter-action dances B may wait till A has stopped moving before reacting but later A and B may overlap each other's phrases.

Inter-action between groups will flourish best when it is based on a foundation of the experiences considered above in this chapter. The teacher can at first direct inter-action between groups. He may say, for instance, that one group must advance towards another group B which will then surround A. Such direction will give the class experiences of interplay between groups but unless scope is left for the groups to improvise their own rhythms or choose their own action they may loose interest. More spontaneous group interplay will emerge when groups working on group motifs travel and encounter other groups. A group which is working on a turning motif may find their turning leads to curved pathways which take them around another group. A number of possibilities will appear to the teacher on the spot as these group encounters arise. Of the actions possible as reactions, the teacher will be able to decide whether a leap, a shrinking away, a sinking, a retreating, a turning away or an addressing gesture would be appropriate. Often the groups themselves only need to be made aware of the encounter and they will be able to react to it when it occurs on the next execution of the motif. The teacher's aim here would be to help bring about continuity of theme. If the theme was a dynamic one, for instance, a group might change its fine touch to a firm touch on encountering another group or change its free flow travelling to bound flow stepping. In this way the teacher would keep the children thinking in dynamic terms rather than spatial or action terms. It is worth stressing however that reacting as a group demands lengthy experience. Frequently it is an individual who first takes initiative and is followed by the rest of the group. This is often as near as a class may get to real group reactions. Once the initial improvisation of the interplay is recalled however, then the group will know what to expect and the reaction will be a group one. But even this situation is difficult and requires intense concentration and empathy among the group members.

Subtleties in relationship

Subtleties in relating to others often arise from a use of the ideas of shadowing and echoing. Shadowing implies imitation of a kind but lacking exactness and absoluteness. One partner may shadow or echo his partner's rising, gesturing, shrinking, jumping, or twisting if the theme was action, shadow or echo his partner's firmness, abandonment, plasticity, or suddenness if the theme was dynamics, and shadow or echo his partner's level, gesture, location, degree of extension, stability or lability or flatness if the theme was concerned with the space.

Form and shape in relationship experiences

When children advance towards a spot or converge on a spot the resulting grouping will take on a form or shape. It may take the formation of a circle, the form of a tightly packed mass or a rounded bunched-up group. This resulting form derives from the mode of approach. A direct approach with linear penetrating type of gesture, or a more roundabout approach where the members drift together and weave their way into their positions will

Plate 1　'The Ballerina' by Amanda, aged 9.

Plate 2 Here the partners work on rising and sinking. One draws upwards with the emphasis on elbows while the other sinks and emphasises the palms. They maintain a steady focus on each other while moving. The body shape for both of these boys is wall-like.

Plate 3 Each pair is working on the movement of circling a partner, while remaining in close to him. The partners might end the phrase by spiralling to the floor into one knotted shape or by leaping apart.

Plate 4 One partner dominates the other. In contrast to plate 2 both boys are here narrow in body shape and using the space in a restricted fashion.

Plate 5 The girls are just beginning the phrase by turning away from each other with a twist. This leads to a turning leap which brings the pair into a facing situation. Each pair had to find their own way of dissolving the confrontation so that the starting position is regained.

Plate 6 The task here is the same as in plate 5. One girl lifts with floating arm gestures and the other traces a curve with her finger tips.

Plate 7   In this task each individual had to find a bunched up position on the floor and hold the position in stony stillness. On the sound of the percussion the body had to unwind as if life was animating the limbs. This boy chose to retain his proximity to the ground and his hand drew smoothly across the floor.

Plate 8 In this phrase the hands had to meet in the zone above the head and then part as the body sinks. This girl soared up into an elongated position in which her feet almost left the ground.

Plate 9   These two boys are improvising on the movement idea of feet touching while on the floor and while in the air. They are each developing a good sense of where the body is in the space.

Plate 10 In this sequence the group had to meet, stay together and then part. The focus here is on the palms but it could also have been on the quality of movement.

Plate 11 This quartet is at the parting stage of the sequence just starting in plate 10. These girls whip apart with three whirling jumps.

Plate 12 In this plate the task was given of approaching a leader and overpowering him.

Plate 13 In this continuation of the theme in plate 12 there is strength and pressure (firm touch) in the sinking movement of some of the boys.

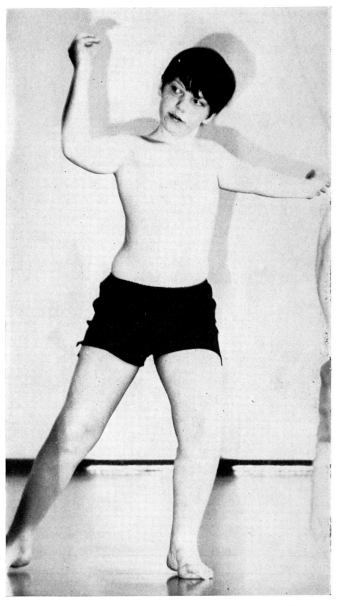

Plate 14 In this plate the theme is body awareness. This boy
is concerned with the action of the elbow.

Plate 15   Here the hands are leading the body into a new situation. Some twist, some sink, and the boy in front is about to rise up. One hand of the boy in front is more active than the other.

Plate 16

Plate 17

Plates 16, 17, 18 and 19 show movements in a sequence concerned with the ideas, unfolding, flying and settling.

Plate 18

Plate 19

each produce different results. The gathering may be achieved by each person arriving at the same time or in a succession. The latter gives each child time to recognise how he may fit into the mass. This is an activity which will be interesting to experienced children but less valuable to the inexperienced.

Some of the richness inherent in group dance will be recognised from the above consideration of relationships which deals with the situations in order of difficulty, beginning with simple shared motifs between class and teacher and ending with encounters and interplays between groups, demanding a high degree of confidence, experience and sensitivity to others. At this point it might help bring back a wider view and reaffirm the role of group dance in education to quote from a lecture by Dr Martin Shipman on *A Sociological Perspective of Dance* (39). He concludes his lecture by saying:

In a world in which each individual must play a number of roles, in a number of different statuses, in a number of organisations dance could serve as an important means of extending the individual's role repertoire. It can not only help prepare the child for interaction with others of different backgrounds, sex, even cultures, it can help bridge the gap between private and public behaviour. Modern society requires public performances in impersonal circumstances and this can be difficult for the insecure. It is here that dance as an early training can serve to prepare individuals to manage the impression they give to others with efficiency and style. The Aboriginal only had to communicate with intimates. Modern man has to associate with a number of different and often strange groups. However efficient the formal schooling the social skills that are necessary in this situation can only come from expressive activities like dance.

SUMMARY

BASIC RELATIONSHIP EXPERIENCES
Class/teacher relationships
Basic group motifs in which the teacher participates with the whole class are the beginning of relationship experience. Contracting to be near the floor followed by extending to be away from the floor is an example of such a motif. Advancing towards the teacher to stop low near to him followed by retreating from the teacher to finish in a space is another.

E

Pair relationships
In all of these beginning stage duos the partners use the same action. The relationship themes include moving together, taking turns, meeting and parting, and follow your leader.

Group experiences
At this early stage, group experiences are concerned with collecting a group and dispersing again.

Transient relationship experiences
These occur when the class is travelling and each individual is weaving in an out of the spaces he can find as he goes.

INTERMEDIATE RELATIONSHIP EXPERIENCES
1. Now duos, trios and small groups can compose using travelling, turning, contracting and extending, and stepping actions for their motifs and phrases in which face-to-face and side-to-side relationships occur.
2. During these explorations awareness of formation becomes increasingly important and many formation changes are gradually absorbed into the child's memory.

MORE ADVANCED RELATIONSHIP EXPERIENCES
1. Whereas previously the same action was used by each person in duos and trios, now each person in the duo or trio may choose his own individual action.
2. At this stage inter-action in twos and threes and later inter-action between groups is developing. With the basic and intermediate work behind them, children show greater sensitivity to each other, together with an ability to anticipate each other's manoeuvres and adapt accordingly.
3. Subtleties in relationship emerge when the children are able to understand and use themes such as 'shadowing'.
4. With accumulating experience in group work the child will begin to be conscious of the patterns of form and shape in changing group formations. Care must be taken here to see that formation results from the action and is not contrived.
5. It is the aim of group work not only to provide opportunities for children to develop social skill but also extend the child's dance vocabulary.

FURTHER READING

North (23): Chapter 5 contains many examples of partner work. Chapter 11 will help the reader to an understanding of more advanced work in groups.

Preston-Dunlop (26): A detailed consideration of partner work will be found in chapter 5. For more advanced work involving trios, quartets, and quintets, see the appendix to the above chapter.

Russell (32 and 33): Both of these books abound with imaginative ideas for group work. (See the index of these books.)

V THE ORGANISATION BY YEAR OF THE SYLLABUS CONTENT

YEAR I

1. *The introduction of action vocabulary*

(*a*) Stepping	*pages*	(24, 25)
(*b*) Travelling		(24)
(*c*) Stopping		(24, 32, 33)
(*d*) Turning		(27)
(*e*) Contraction and extension		(25, 26)
(*f*) Hand gestures		(28, 29, 30)
(*g*) Jumping		(26, 27)

2. *The introduction of body awareness*

(*a*) Hands and feet	*pages*	(28, 30)
(*b*) Elbows and knees		(30)

3. *The introduction of spatial awareness*

Orientation with reference to

(*a*) The body centre	*pages*	(45, 46)
(*b*) The floor		(46, 47)
(*c*) The parts of the body		(47)
(*d*) A partner		(47, 48)

4. *The introduction of dynamic awareness*

(*a*) The motion factor of flow	*pages*	(24, 37)

(b) The motion factor of weight   *pages* (37)
(c) The motion factor of time   (19, 38, 39)

5. *The introduction of relationship*
   (a) Class/teacher relationships   *pages* (56, 57)
   (b) Partner work   (57, 58)
   (c) Group work   (59)

YEAR 2

1. *Development of action vocabulary*
1. Continuing experience of the action material in YEAR 1

2. *Action combinations*
    (i) Turning while jumping   *pages* (26, 27, 28)
   (ii) Contracting while turning   (25–28)
  (iii) Contracting while twisting   (25, 26, 28–30)
   (iv) Extending while turning   (25–28)
    (v) Extending while twisting   (25, 26, 28–30)
   (vi) Extending while jumping   (25–28)
  (vii) Jumping while gesturing   (26, 27, 29, 30)
 (viii) Jumping while twisting and gesturing (26, 27, 29, 30)
   (ix) Turning while gesturing   (27–30)
    (x) Extending while gesturing   (25, 26, 28–30)
   (xi) Contracting while gesturing   (25, 26, 28–30)

3. *Development of body awareness*
1. Continuing experience in YEAR 1 material
2. Leading with parts of the body   *pages* (29, 30)

4. *Development of spatial awareness*
1. Continuing experience in YEAR 1 material
2. Placing movement in zones
   (a) Above   *pages* (48, 49)
   (b) Below   (48, 49)
   (c) In front   (48, 49)
   (d) Behind   (48, 49)
   (e) At the side   (48, 49)
3. Scale   (49, 50)

5. *Development of dynamic awareness*
1. Continuing experience in YEAR 1 material
2. The motion factor of flow   *pages* (37)
3. Weight and time combinations   (40)

6. *Development of the ability to relate to others*
1. Continuing experience in YEAR 1 material
2. Trios   *pages* (61–63)

YEAR 3
1. *Development of action vocabulary*
1. Consolidation in YEAR 1 and YEAR 2 work
2. Arm and leg gesture   *pages* (31, 32)

2. *Development of body awareness*
1. Consolidation in YEAR 1 and YEAR 2 work
2. Guidances   *pages* (29)
3. Relationship of parts of the body in stillness and in
   action (e.g. shape)   (32, 33, 50–52)

3. *Development of spatial awareness*
1. Consolidation in YEAR 1 and YEAR 2 work
2. Pathways   *pages* (53, 54)

4. *Development of dynamic awareness*
1. Consolidation in YEAR 1 and YEAR 2 work
2. Combinations of motion factors   *pages* (39, 40)
3. (*a*) Weight and flow combinations   (41)
   (*b*) Space and time combinations   (41)

5. *Development of the ability to relate to others*
1. Consolidation in YEAR 1 and YEAR 2 work
2. Formation plays   *pages* (65–67)
3. Group inter-action   (65–67)

YEAR 4
1. *Development of action vocabulary*
   The mastery of vocabulary already experienced in YEARS 1, 2
   and 3

E2

2. *Development of body awareness*
1. The mastery of YEAR 1, 2 and 3 work
2. Hip and chest regions   *pages* (31, 32)

3. *Development of spatial awareness*
1. The mastery of YEAR 1, 2 and 3 work
2. Lability and stability   *pages* (52, 53)

4. *Development of dynamic awareness*
1. The mastery of YEAR 1, 2 and 3 work
2. Combinations of motion factors
   (*a*) Space and flow combinations   *pages* (40, 41)
   (*b*) Space and weight combinations   (41, 42)
   (*c*) Flow and time combinations   (42)

5. *Development of ability to relate to others*
1. Further experience in YEAR 1, 2 and 3 work
2. Trios, quartets, quintets   *pages* (64–67)

3 The roles of the Teacher

The teacher's work as organiser begins in practice with the supervision of the preliminary class activity of changing into dance 'kit' and moving from the classroom to the hall. The establishment of an efficient routine at this stage contributes to the formation of good working attitudes and gives the teacher a good opportunity for assessing the mood of the class. From this assessment the teacher will be able to decide upon an appropriate way of introducing the first activity of the lesson, an important one in motivating the class. The functions of the first activity are expressed clearly by Joan Russell in *Creative Dance in the Secondary School* (33, p. 87). She writes:

The first activity of the lesson serves to bridge the gap between the lessons, usually a week apart; it serves to integrate a class which may be made up of pupils not normally working together, often the case when two classes are put together for dance; it may warm up the group in cold weather . . . should aim to bring the group into the mood for movement and be in the nature of a relaxing and loosening activity.

It will be found that the involvement of the class, achieved through the initial activity, may be maintained when the lesson material is organised so that a balance is struck between the following contrasting experiences: locomotory activities and activities which are confined to the spot; energetic activities and calm activities; and lastly individual activities and group activities.

The lesson conclusion must also be considered. The teacher may organise the lesson material so that the conclusion becomes either the climax point or the moment for calming activities.

A consideration of the organisation of the dance lesson would be incomplete without some thought for the creativity of the child. The plan of the lesson must also envisage situations in which the child can succeed in creative work independently of the teacher. Situations which offer such scope to the child may be seen in the sample lessons described later in this chapter.

THE TEACHER AS OBSERVER

Once the lesson has begun and the children are engaged in action the teacher's observations will be influential in forming his subsequent comment on the children's movement responses, his questions, and his further choice of movement activities. Thus teaching dance is seen to be in part an improvisation consisting of intuitive inter-action between teacher and class and not merely a stimulus/response situation.

The teacher's observations will also guide him in deciding how far he can press a class or an individual towards movement mastery at any particular time. No amount of pressure to improve will be effective if it is untimely.

THE TEACHER AS ADVISER

The cultivation of an appreciative attitude to the efforts of the class is an important attribute of the teacher in his role as adviser. The first response must be recognised and praised in such a way that attention is drawn to those characteristics of the response which are to be encouraged. If a child makes a well-controlled finish to a sequence for example then the teacher may say 'Good, that's a well-controlled finish'. In this way the attention of the rest of the class is drawn to this important characteristic of the response. A positive attitude such as this, which encourages improvement by recognising success, is preferable to a negative attitude which does not encourage improvement but demonstrates disapproval of failure. The danger in a negative approach is underlined by Joan Russell in her book already referred to, *Creative Dance in the Secondary School* (33, p. 87):

The nature of dance, with the requirement of full participation on the part of the class, is such that an approach which is negative or which suggests that the response is 'wrong' will be fatal to the establishment of a climate in which creative work can develop.

At those moments in the dance lesson when repetition is being used in order to master a particular action or sequence, the teacher in his capacity as adviser must ensure that with each repetition there is a fresh objective set. In repeating a sequence of movement for instance, the class may be set the task of aiming for rhythmic precision, or smooth transitions between each phrase or clear dynamics.

THE TEACHER AS ACCOMPANIST

In addition to the objectives considered above it is necessary to consider the specific role of the teacher as accompanist. The teacher's aims in this respect are to give rhythmic support to the class activities and at appropriate times to give cues for starting and stopping. Suitable rhythmic accompaniment helps to give security and binds the class together in the common rhythm. Action words such as 'jump', 'travel', 'turn', 'rise', 'sink', 'go', 'stop', 'stamp' and 'patter' may be spoken as an accompaniment. Football crowds demonstrate how words may be spoken rhythmically. Perhaps chanted is a better word than spoken in this context. The use of words to accompany dance is a feature of Balinese dance technique. In *Dance and Drama in Bali*, Beryl de Zoete describes a dance teacher's accompaniment (4, p. 31):

He sang melodies and accentuated rhythms with a succession of syllables: dédolàr – dédelèr – nínong – nénongnèr, not – ndong – ne – not – ndong, nang – nderongrongrong, and many other lively combinations, reproducing the rhythm of drum and cymbals; for the children had only been learning three days, and were feeling their way into the steps and movements.

Clapping is another effective form of accompaniment which can be used in conjunction with the voice or independently.

Both starting together and stopping together intensify class effort and help establish an alert and active mood. Suitable starting cues are: 'ready ... *go*'; 'ready ... *and*'; 'prepare ... and ... *go*'. Whatever the words chosen happen to be, the first part of the cue is a preparation signal and the last part is the starting signal. When the teacher is definite in cueing the activities the class will feel secure.

SCHEMES OF WORK AND LESSON PLANNING

If the teacher has a class of children regularly for a term, then a straightforward scheme of work might include material concerned with action, dynamics, space, and relationship. Such a scheme of work is shown in Table 1. There are five parts, A (action), B (body awareness), R (relationship), D (dynamics), and S (space).

TABLE I

A
Action
Travelling, turning,
jumping, twisting,
contracting, extending,
stopping, stepping

B
Body Awareness
Whole body participation
use of feet, hands,
elbows and knees

R
Relationship
Teacher/class relationship
Partner work
Gathering a group
leading and following
Meeting and parting

D
Dynamics
The motion factors
of time, flow and
weight
Time/weight combinations

S
Space
Awareness of the
body centre
Levels – high and low
Size of movement
Filling space

All lessons would include material from A, B, and R, and in each single lesson material would also be chosen from *either* D or S. In this case the teacher has to keep four aspects of movement in mind. The four might be A, B, R and D or A, B, R and S. At certain times during the lesson the emphasis may fall on action and body awareness, or action and relationship, or action and dynamics, or body awareness and relationship, or body awareness and dynamics.

SAMPLE LESSONS

The following examples of dance lessons are put forward so that the reader may see how material may be selected from the scheme, Table 1, and used in the lesson.

Lesson 1

TABLE 2

A	B	R
Travelling	Whole body	Individual work
Stopping	participation	Partner work
	Feet	
	S	
	High level	
	Deep level	

Travelling is the first activity in this lesson. Most of the children may respond with running steps but the teacher must look for variation and be appreciative of it. Time will be allowed for practice in stopping, and the class's attention may be drawn to the rhythmic sound patterns made by the action of the feet on the floor. Importance could be given to being able to 'hold the position' on the teacher's signal to stop. The teacher's questions could focus attention on these positions and as body awareness in this lesson is concerned with feet the questions addressed to the class might require the child to observe which part of the foot touches the floor and whether both feet or one only bears the weight of the body. One child may have the whole sole of the foot firmly planted on the floor, while another child rests lightly on his toes. Exploration of the movement of the feet in making contact with the ground and in bearing the weight of the body in travelling and in stance will be emphasised in this lesson.

After an unsettling activity such as travelling, in which there is a continued shift from one spot to another, an activity which keeps each child in one spot will be a welcome contrast. The movement involved in changing from high positions where the body is extended to low positions near the floor will be effective in bringing about this contrast.

If the teacher can make a smooth transition from the travelling activity to the 'on the spot' activity the flow of the lesson will be maintained. It will be possible to make a smooth transition in this case by stressing the level of the body positions. When the class is practising 'stops' and the last stop has to be in a low-level position, then the teacher can introduce the action of rising. These rising actions may vary from the whole body calmly extending upwards, to springing up off the floor giving the impression of exploding into the air. At this stage in the lesson the teacher should be able to observe variety in the children's response and may use the variations of particular children as a stimulus to further exploration.

After working to master these activities the children might work in pairs to build a sequence composed of travelling stopping and rising, and returning to the floor. Each short duo may be distinguished by some particular feature. For example the singularity of one duo may be due to an emphasis on symmetry.

While the children work on their duos the teacher will be free to circulate in order to give help and encouragement.

In this lesson the completing of the sequences would bring about a satisfying conclusion.

Lesson 2

TABLE 3

A	B
Jumping	Proximity to the
Turning	floor of parts of the
Travelling	body

R	D
Individual work	Firm touch
Partner work	Fine touch
	Flow

The class might be asked in this lesson to use lots of space by travelling and jumping. Phrases such as 'Let me see your jumps filling the space' will encourage purposeful movement.

After the expansive character of this first activity it will be possible to set the task of going and stopping, using small jumps in which the feet stay near the floor. The emphasis here may be placed on readiness to stop so that bound flow jumps are encouraged. Since both of these jumping activities stir up excitement, it would be appropriate to introduce a calm activity next. Such an activity might be: changing with fine touch from deep positions near the floor to high positions and returning to the floor again with firm touch. The dynamic theme of this lesson is stressed by demanding increase of tension in the downward action towards the floor and decrease of tension in the rising up again.

It will be possible to introduce partner relationship when each child has had an opportunity to both explore and master this lesson material. Each pair may now be asked to make their own sequence in which firm touch in moving together down to the floor is contrasted with fine touch in rising up from the floor. When the children have had an opportunity to complete this task they may be asked to find a way to separate using turning jumps. This final jumping activity would bring these sequences to a climax. Observation of each other's sequences would be a possible way to conclude the lesson.

Lesson 3

TABLE 4

A	B
Travelling	Whole body
Extending	participation –
Contracting	elbows, palms, trunk

R	D
Teacher/class	Firm touch
group movement	Fine touch
relating to a	Time-incidental flow –
leader	careful stepping and free
	flow travelling.

This lesson might begin with the class grouped closely about the teacher. To gain concentration a specific starting position might be set, such as crouching with both hands touching the floor. The first task might consist of extending slowly into an elongated position and contracting to return to the starting situation again. During this activity the teacher may continually ask for clarity by setting aims or posing questions. He may, for example, use any of the following phrases: 'Show clearly which hand leads', 'Be bound in flow and smooth in the contraction'. Such phrases will stimulate awareness, and lead to clarity in movement and quality and rhythm. The children's individuality will show in their response to these accompanying phrases. For example, one child may contract more on one side of the body than the other and thus arrive in pleasing asymmetric positions.

If elbows lead the extension and contraction then twists and asymmetric movement will result. Leading with the elbow would be helpful in making the contraction forceful while leading with the finger tips would be helpful in making the extension fine touch in quality.

Travelling will be a good contrasting activity to follow the more static activity of contracting and extending. The class might first retreat from the teacher and then advance towards him. Other possible interplays between the teacher and class might include:

1. The teacher retreats and the class advances.
2. The teacher travels to a spot and stops. Then the class follows.

Variation in the flow and part of the body leading could be made in these variations.

The middle section of this lesson could now be precipitated by giving five children each a tambour or tambourine and asking the class to divide up into five groups, each group to join a person who has a tambourine. The first task might then consist of a travelling and stopping in which the group follow the leader.

The teacher can, at this stage in the lesson, circulate from group to group. He may now help groups to achieve more clarity in dynamics, encourage, and make appreciative comment.

When these sequences are well under way the teacher may then set the class the final task of ending the sequence with a group motif consisting of contracting and extending.

SUMMARY

1. As organiser the teacher supervises the class in 'changing' and in moving between the changing room and the hall; organises lesson material so that movement activities are balanced; and sets up situations in which children may achieve success in independent creative work.
2. The teacher allows his observation to guide him in selecting activities; formulating questions; in commenting on the children's response; and in judging the degree of movement mastery possible at any particular time.
3. As adviser the teacher cultivates an appreciative attitude to the efforts of the class; encourages learning by rewarding success; and demands movement repetition only when it is meaningful.
4. As accompanist the teacher provides rhythmic support for the class activities, and gives the cues for the beginning and end of activities.
5. In the scheme of work discussed in this chapter, equal importance is given to action and body awareness; dynamics, the use of space, partner and group work.
6. The sample lessons illustrate how material may be selected from the scheme and developed in the lesson.

FURTHER READING

Russell (32) contains a chapter on 'The Teacher's Task' in the dance lesson.

North (23, p. 62): Here there is a section on the teacher's role. This whole chapter will prove valuable in considering the dance lesson.

4 Making Dances

A teacher will learn to help children to compose their own dances through practice in the dance lesson, rather than through the study of any written guide but there *are* three principles of composition worth bearing in mind. These are:

1. Repetition
2. Sequence
3. Climax.

Repetition

Paintings and sculptures are durable but dances are transient. Each performance of the dance is a new beginning, never exactly identical to the one before. There is no doubt that painters and sculptors derive satisfaction from knowing that their successful works will last. No such satisfaction is possible for the dancer, for in dancing the artefact has long life only in a good memory and even a *good* memory needs reviving from time to time. Because of this short-lived nature of the movement experience, the dancer makes use of repetition.

Repetition is particularly important for children who are learning to compose their own dances. The motif is a small enough unit to be easily remembered and through repetition it is made more memorable and given clarity. It is from this first building stone that the composition must grow and the more vivid the experience of the basic motif the better are the chances for a good development. However, the child must be guided in his repetitions towards a knowledge of the import of the motif. To know the import of a movement means deciding from the repeated experience of it whether the dynamic aspect and spatial aspect are equally important or whether one aspect is stressed. Movements with a spatial stress would include: unfolding and folding, swooping and hovering, rising and dipping, enclosing and containing, making a pathway, penetrating and cutting through space, sweeping and pinpointing, confronting, withdrawing, and approaching, overbalancing and stabilising, sinking and spreading, and shrinking and growing. Movements with a dynamic stress would include: exploding and settling, flinging and falling, pressing downwards, gently stepping high, scurrying, stamping, and whipping gestures and grinding turns.

In addition to these considerations the way in which the parts of the body relate to each other must be appreciated. They may relate in a variety of ways. For example, there may be counterpoint, harmony, symmetry, and asymmetry.

When inventing motifs to repeat it is helpful at first if the last movement returns to the beginning position. Good movement ideas for such motifs are closing and opening, rising and sinking, swaying and turning, jumping and travelling, stepping and stopping, contracting and extending, and advancing and retreating.

In a sequence of movement incorporating several motifs, repeating any one of these brings added significance to this part of the sequence. Of course a repetition need not immediately follow the first statement of a motif. A different motif may come between the first statement and the repeat. This would produce an A B A pattern. Other permutations would include: A A B A, A B B A, A B A A, A A B A A A.

Sequence
In a good movement sequence each movement grows out of the preceding one. This growth may be experienced when extensions lead to elevation; overbalancing leads to travelling and stabilising; twisting leads to turning or untwisting; confined small-range movement leads to expansive movement; movement near the floor leads to rising; or gesture leads to contracting, extending, turning, leaping, or travelling.

There are three organic rhythms which are important in building a sequence. These rhythms are called impact, impulse and swing.

Impactive rhythms take the form of preparation and result. For example, we may leap to enjoy the impact with the floor; withdraw in preparation for thrusting out; gesture across the body in preparation for an opening slapping gesture; or rise up to tower above the floor before stamping down again. Impulsive rhythms are characterised by an explosive start followed by a gradual petering out of movement. For example, an impulsive expansion may melt into a shrinking combined with several stabilising steps; an explosive leap will peter out in a travelling recovery; a movement which begins with an impulsive toss of the head which brings the whole body upwards with a degree of twist will be able to peter out in a downwards spiralling.

In swinging rhythms the accent falls in the middle of the movement. Examples of this rhythm include large pendulum movements from side to side in which the arms swing from one point of an arc to the other. When the whole body participates there is a giving-in to gravity in the fall of the swing and a rising action at each end of the swing. Other examples include swinging movements which have a forwards and backwards orientation and centrifugal swings where the arms circle from the shoulder. The circling may be in a horizontal plane or in a plane tilted off the horizontal. The waltz has a swinging rhythm, brought about in a rising and sinking step pattern. A gathering gesture followed by a scattering gesture will fall into a swing rhythm. The gathering gesture may swing inwards towards or across the body centre and scatter outwards with either a leap, several travelling steps or a turn.

A good understanding of the first movement in a sequence precipitates the act of sensing an appropriate movement to follow it. This kind of understanding is developed through the exploration of bodily action considered in Sections I, II and III of Chapter 2, and when it is combined with a rhythmic sense based on the above organic patterns, a good foundation is laid for composing sequences.

Climax

A control of climax gives added meaning to sequences. The climax point may be at the beginning, middle or end of a section.

Each of these possibilities will have its own particular expression. A dance sequence where the climax is at the beginning immediately alerts the body and the dénouement gradually or abruptly relaxes it. The climax point is at the beginning in each of the following examples.

The first sequence explodes with forceful turning jumps and crouching movements. This opening leads to medium-level spinning which tapers into a slow smooth travelling finish.

In this second sequence the beginning section opens with a striding motif which takes the body with a rush through the space to a definite focus. The feet reach out in the striding steps bringing the legs into full extension as a result. A retreat from this focus using medium-sized steps leads to a final drawing together of the feet while the whole body shrinks.

In the first sequence the climax is dissolved through a gradual change to more harmonious movement. The further change from the extreme contrast of elevation and deep-level movement to the steady use of the medium level also contributes to the falling off from the climax. The fall from the climax in the second sequence is achieved through decrease in size of steps plus the gradual change from the outward going action of striding to the inward looking action of shrinking. Both sequences have a decrease in speed and forcefulness towards the end.

The more dramatic nature of this third example, a duo, may be accounted for by the placing of the partners in relationship to each other and the emphasis on the weight factor. They begin their duo from a back to back situation from which they spring into a leaping turn to land confronting each other. They approach each other with firm deliberate steps, strongly link elbows (without any decrease in tension) and circle each other. During the circling they gradually sink down towards the floor while dissolving their link. A slow sliding gesture takes each partner onto the floor to finish.

When the climax point is in the middle of the sequence each movement from the beginning will usually lead towards this central peak and each subsequent movement will contribute to the fall away. The following three examples have this pattern.

In the first sequence the compactness of a group waxes and

wanes by each member making a withdrawing gesture from the group centre and an advancing gesture towards it again. The gesture grows in size until each member is travelling some distance from the centre and then rushing back to it. The increase in size and speed reaches its climax through each group member arriving at the centre with a rush and leap. The sequence ends with a gentle and calm gesture away from the central focus, a gesture towards it again and a final gesture away which takes each member into a turn to end alone and in a space.

The second sequence is more playful in character and has the relationship of the hands and knees as a central theme. Each child starts in a deep position with his right hand on his right knee and his left hand on his left knee. The trunk is supported by the hands resting on the knees. From stillness each child sways from side to side so that each foot lifts off the ground with each sway. During this grotesque movement the hands remain on the knees as if stuck. The sway develops into a lumbering skipping kind of jump which takes on the rhythm tee-tum, tee-tum, tee-tum-tum. On the last tum-tum the landing is on two feet and contrasts in its stability with the rollicking rocking of the skipping. The hands still grasp the knees as if stuck fast. At the end of the repeat of this jumping motif there is a pause. This pause is broken by a repeated pulling heaving action as if the hands are trying to break their contact with the knees. The progress of this sequence culminates with the sudden release of the hands from the knees. A whirling and leaping dance immediately celebrates the hands' freedom. On the landing from the last jump the hands become stuck again and the dance finished with a slow repeat of the early rocking walk.

In this third example, a duo, the climax is reached when the partners dance together near to each other. Each dancer begins with an opening movement to one side led by the elbow, continues with a similar gesture on the other side and on a repeat of the gesture on the original side is led into a turning pathway which brings him alongside his partner to link elbows. The pair retain their link in a lively rhythmic motif involving jumps and steps. The partners then separate and a return to the earlier opening motif ends the sequence. The rhythmic climax of the central section is sandwiched between the lyrical beginning and ending sections.

A definite sense of completion may be given to a sequence when the climax comes at the end. The following descriptions are of sequences with climaxes at the end. In this first sequence the development towards the climax is spatial. A slow on-the-spot motif with contained gestures, restricted in their use of space, gives way to a turning motif characterised by broader, wider-ranging gestures which lead to travelling. The travelling includes expansive turning jumps which fill the space. The last jump leads to a final high position with arms outspread.

The second example consists of a meeting and parting theme for a group in which the build-up to the climax is a rhythmic one. The group is compact to begin with and the members repeatedly withdraw and return with step variations to this compact formation. With each return the rhythm of the stepping intensifies until the final return when the meeting culminates in a stamping motif with a final thrusting gesture on the last stamp.

In the last example the sequence has a playful character and proceeds in a narrative form, one event leading to another towards the final peak. One child enters the space and establishes himself in a low position. Three children now enter cautiously advancing in a wall formation, grasping each other's hands. They stop before the first child who jumps up and travels across the room in zigzag pathways. Each of his changes of direction is caused by the other three children who cut him off. These three succeed in catching the first child after several zigzags and encircle him to capture him. The circle is just about to squeeze in on the central child when he darts out under the arms of two children in the circle and races to a space of his own to face in a mocking position the three surprised partners.

During early stages in composition work it is a helpful plan to set tasks in which short sequences with one climax only have to be built. When it is clear from observation that the children have some mastery in control of climax then longer sequences with more than one climax may be attempted.

In almost all of the examples given above progress towards

and away from the climax was gradual but it is possible for the progress to be abrupt and uneven when appropriate.

STIMULI FOR DANCE

1. *Movement*

Movement itself is the richest source of subject matter for dances. For example, dances may grow out of movement ideas such as: jumping, travelling and turning, the qualities of firm touch and fine touch, the spatial contrast of high and deep movement, and meeting and withdrawing from a partner. These examples sound abstract to some but they are certainly not abstract to the child who jumps, exerts his strength in action, or sinks down to the floor. To him these ideas are references to real experiences.

No further consideration of this theme is undertaken here since Chapter 2 deals with this subject matter.

2. *Literature*

Poetry, fairy tales, the Bible and the novel may all be considered under this heading.

Rhythm is a vital element common to both poetry and dance and for this reason these arts have a close affinity. Poems like 'Sea Fever' by Masefield will stimulate dance in which the rhythms of wind and water may be reflected in movement which rises, falls, comes to a climax and ebbs. The movement rhythms associated with the pluck of the wind and the pull of the tides may be embodied in movement by swaying, whirling, sudden turning leaps and quick gestures which snatch the body into the air. There are images in 'Sea Fever' which conjure up vast open spaces and others which bring to mind small cosy spaces. In movement this contrast may be felt in broad open gestures and contained gestures of small extent.

'The Second Coming' by W. B. Yeats (36) is a poem which would be suitable for group dance of a very dramatic nature. Another poem of Yeats, 'The Stolen Child', would be suitable for a dance involving an individual, and a group which lures the individual away from the real world. The imagery in this poem suggests calm, lyrical dance and vigorous leaping dance.

'hist whist' by e. e. cummings (31) is a comic and lively poem with very stimulating rhythms, and would lead to playful dance which included stepping, sharp crisp contractions and extensions, and little jumps.

All of these poems could be spoken as the accompaniment to the dance interpretations which could use the verse rhythms and vocal dynamics of the reader as music.

Witch themes have an appeal for all ages. The witches' chant from *Macbeth* would make a strong rhythmic accompaniment to a circular dance in which each individual steps and leaps. To bring out the characterisation in movement, elbows, wrists, hands and knees could come into play, creating grotesque angularity.

The novel is a rich source of subject matter for characterisation in dance. The Queen of Narnia in C. S. Lewis' novel *The Lion, the Witch and the Wardrobe*, for example, would make a good subject for work of this kind. Her character has an evil grandeur as well as a serpent-like craftiness. Deep-level movement which hugs the ground like a beast, high-level sharp gestures which bring the whole body into tall stances and gestures in which the limbs rotate and twist the body will all help in exploring this character.

Biblical characters such as Joseph, Nebuchadnezzar, Saul, Samson and the Apostle Paul are good subjects for dance characterisation. Each of them experiences dramatic changes in circumstances. For example, Samson is helpless in his blindness and triumphant in his death; Saul is heroic and proud in battle but tortured when overtaken by the evil spirit; Nebuchadnezzar is mighty as a king but lowly as a beast-like creature; Paul is changed by his conversion from being a hunter of Christians to a Christian himself.

The authority of Nebuchadnezzar the King might be explored in symmetrical rising actions and commanding opening and closing gestures. The ferocity of Nebuchadnezzar the soldier might be explored through forceful leaping, stalking steps, strong sudden advances, and firm gestures that lead to opening rising and leaping. The beast-like Nebuchadnezzar might be explored through deep movement comprising crouching, swaying, prowling steps, and clawing gestures.

The adolescent will be more able to capture the moods connected with the characters' change in circumstances while the junior child will be more preoccupied with the actions of the character in a sequence of events such as Saul in battle or Nebuchadnezzar stalking.

Fairy tales and legends are a further source of subject matter for dance. The contrasting movement experiences of nimble stepping and jumping, and broad big sweeping gestures, turns, and striding steps would be a good introduction to short little sequences characterising Peter Pan and Captain Hook.

When the teacher sees that the class understands the movement traits of two characters he will then be able to introduce situations in which one character relates in dance to another. For example, after working on movement characterising Peter Pan and Captain Hook, partner dances may show the nimble Peter 'dancing rings round' the slower Captain Hook. When the class has had several experiences involving pairs, trios, or a group, then more freedom may be given to the class in choosing the relationship situation and the action which takes place in this situation.

3. *The world of nature*

Our sense of dynamics is stirred by the rhythmic movement of natural phenomena. Words like exploding, folding, unfolding, swaying, bursting, whirlpooling and floating may stimulate individual improvisation, or group inventions.

The associations that the four elements, fire, water, earth and air, have for man are closely linked with movement. Both musicians and poets have been inspired by this theme. T. S. Eliot's *Four Quartets* is a famous example.

The following lists of words will be useful in stimulating movement explorations on the elements. Flickering, darting and leaping are associated with fire. Flowing, gushing, meandering, whirling are associated with water. Pushing, driving, plucking, floating, soaring, drifting, whirling are associated with air. Heaving, erupting, splitting are associated with earth. The movement explorations resulting from these words may be carried out by each child working individually, by pairs or by groups of children. Some words will be more suitable for group sequences.

The inter-action of the elements is a further possibility for dance work involving groups. For example, a group inter-action might comprise a gentle swaying water group which is stirred into travelling and whirling by the driving force of an air group.

Dance improvisation may also be stimulated by the following movement ideas associated with animals, birds, and insects; galloping, rearing, bouncing, flying, hovering, swooping, gliding, contracting and curling, undulating, leaping, clawing, stampeding, pouncing and soaring.

These associations may be merely starting points from which little dances and dance dramas may grow. From working on movement, characteristic of birds, a dance drama may grow up around the idea of the birds and the bird-catchers. Exploration of the bird-catcher's movement could take the form of prowling steps, scanning gestures, and pouncing jumps. The resulting dance drama might be organised as a duo or as a play between a group and an individual. There might, for instance, be a group which represents the hunter. The group might then capture the bird by surrounding it so that the bird appeared to vanish within the group circle. The circle might then become a cage-like barrier from which the individual aims to escape.

When the groups have worked out their sequence then time will need to be spent on clarification. This will bring the groups to a point in the lesson when they look objectively at their work. A helpful direction is given to some groups' thoughts when they are asked to see that their sequence has a clear beginning, middle and end.

The first dance dramas may have only one definite incident with one climax point while at a later stage there may be several incidents and minor climaxes relating to the major climax.

The teacher should be prepared to follow the directions of development suggested by the class's response to his initial stimulus. It might happen that after a lesson introduction concerned with the elements of fire and water, certain aspects of the movement may become the central preoccupation of the children and the initial stimulus may be discarded. The teacher may feel that it is worth while to encourage the class to build the composition around this preoccupation even when it means allowing the

F

initial stimulus to be forgotten. Though in this case the initial stimulus has already served a valuable purpose in extending the class's experience.

4. *Ritual*

Ritual in the form of movement patterns concerned with worship are suitable sources of subject matter for dances. Rising and elevating actions may form the basis of dances of praise. The dynamic expression may be energetic and joyful or calm and serene. Actions of kneeling, bowing, closing, and travelling towards a focal point and around a focal point may form the basis of dances of prayer. The dynamic expression may arise from firm or fine touch, sustainment, and symmetrical groupings or take a contrasting expression arising from whirling rhythmic gathering actions, and sudden and strong gestures which may result in elevation. Interest in the rituals of such peoples as the Balinese, the North American Indians, and the Aztecs may arise from work in geography and lead to dance.

5. *Voice Sound*

Children at play give voice to the run of their imaginations with a great variety of humming, buzzing, hissing, and explosive sounds. The lips vibrate with engine sounds and from the throat issue a variety of sounds which we could describe with words such as hoarse, shrill, croaking, soft, and hard. These sounds vary in pitch, duration, and volume, and produce rhythms which are infinitely varied and expressive. Hardly any sounds are voiced in stillness. The whole body stirs with movement which unfolds or erupts with the sound, and the variety and expressiveness of the movement is as great as that of the sound. In the dance lesson, not to use such a flexible and expressive instrument as the voice would be neglectful indeed. No sound instrument is more immediate to the child or as much under his control as the voice.

In the first attempts at movement with vocal accompaniment, it will be helpful to the class to stimulate movement first and when the children have established a movement phrase or confidently made several movement improvisations, then to set the sound task. The task might be 'Now, with your voice, make your own sound for the movement', or 'Now, with voice sounds accompany your own movement'.

It will also be found helpful if the exploration of voice sound as an activity has been established in the classroom so that the child's awareness and control of the repertoire of possible sounds is developed. Such exploration may be part of work in poetry, music, or drama.

Simple movement tasks such as whole body actions of sinking and rising will allow the child to concentrate on the sound accompaniment and the combination of sound and movement. When the lesson is progressing in a happy climate of play, sound and movement will evolve together of course. A great number of dynamic variations may be found in exploring any simple task. In rising and sinking actions, for instance, a slow sinking accompanied by a glissando-like descending hum may break into a sudden rise with a high pitched *whee-e-e*, a strong sinking action in which tension gathers may be accompanied by a deep *err-r-r* sound which accelerates into a *i-i-p-pp* sound as the body shoots upwards, or a sudden sinking to a percussive closed *zzip* sound may lead to a sustained rise to a steady open sound.

The possibilities multiply considerably when the explorations of the child include work with a partner or a group. In partner work, activities such as doing the same, and follow the leader will make suitable beginning tasks. The rising and sinking motifs described above, for example, may be carried out in pairs. In follow the leader tasks in which the action is rising and sinking, one partner may easily follow the sound and action of the leader since the bodily action involved is very simple. More complex results will occur when rising and sinking actions are included in tasks requiring action and reaction in pairs. Here one partner may sink calmly with a steady hum to be answered by his partner who spins up with a *whee-e-e* sound from a crouch position.

The expressive possibilities of overlapping sounds will soon be discovered by the children while working on tasks such as the above. Such discovery will pave the way towards a full exploration of sounds in combinations which will be possible in group work. Group motifs in which sound accompanies the movement will result from tasks which require group actions of meeting and parting, circling, travelling, and rising and sinking. Many more activities suitable for groups will be found in Chapter 2, Section IV. In these tasks, sound dynamics such as the following may be explored: crescendo and diminuendo, continuous sound contrasted with interrupted sound, and long-sustained sounds contrasted with single accentuated sounds. Textural variations may be discovered by exploring, for example, closed hard sounds such as some consonants against open soft sounds such as some of the vowels. Rich textures will also arise from hard sounds and soft sounds in combination.

Even further variety will result when sound texture and sound volume are both explored in the same sound composition. In all of these explorations it will be found that sound and movement will interact, one inspiring the other in a reciprocal relationship.

Work of the kind described above will lead to the use of words. When this happens new inspiration will result from the meanings attached to the words. In this event the words chosen can be selected for their relevance to a theme. 'The Wind', for example, could result in a grouping of words which included roar, whine, whistle, blow, breeze, breath, rushing, mighty, drifting, windswept, cold, flap, gust, force and many more. The variety of sounds which are included in this word list is considerable and it is easy to see that a little orchestration organised by the teacher would readily produce sound compositions of very varied mood, all inspiring pieces for dance.

Children use their voices freely in play and they will also use them freely in the dance lesson provided the teacher creates a congenial atmosphere in which the spirit of play is felt. All classes in Middle School will be enriched by the use of voice sound, but the older the class the more sensitive to class mood the teacher will have to be, when he comes to introduce work of this kind. In introducing voice sound work to older classes, he will be wise to wait for an opportunity when the class is particularly responsive and a good class/teacher relationship is felt.

6. *Percussion*

Gongs, cymbals, triangles, and indian-bells produce long-lasting sounds which may be cut short by pressing the fingers on the vibrating surface. Drums produce a short-lived sound which may be varied in pitch. Playing near the centre of the drum skin produces a deep pitch and playing near the edge produces a higher pitch. When beaters are used to play these instruments, the hardness or softness of the beater will influence the character of sound produced. Maraccas, school castanets, and sleighbells produce sound of short duration unless they are continuously shaken. The tambourine produces the most varied sounds of all.

Gongs and cymbals may stimulate expanding and shrinking actions, broad movement, and explosive movement that gradually peters out. Triangles and indian-bells may stimulate gentle sinking, rising, travelling and sustained delicate gesture. Drums may stimulate sharp leaps, stepping and travelling. Rhythm sticks and skulls and castanets may stimulate sudden little jumps, darting steps and gestures and sharp brilliant turns. Maraccas and sleighbells may stimulate whirling, scurrying steps, swinging gestures, and little bouncy jumps. Tambourines, the most versatile of the percussion instruments, may stimulate dynamic variations of all the five bodily actions.

Percussion sounds will be particularly effective in stimulating and reinforcing movement dynamics. Short little sequences may be crystallised from exploratory beginnings. Initially the teacher may play the instruments while the children respond individually or in groups, but at a later stage each group might then respond to the sound of one instrument which is played by a member of the group. This member should be encouraged to participate as fully in the group movement as the instrument will allow. Tambourines, maraccas, bells and castanets have the advantage of being easy to play while dancing. In fact, the bells can be fixed to the ankles for dancing.

7. *Music*

For many people, dance is inseparably linked in their minds with music. This fact is not surprising when one remembers that dance performances without a music accompaniment are the exception. In our classical music we still have the minuet section of the symphony and the classical suite which reminds us of the close relationship between dance and music.

However, it is a mistake to think that dance in education must always be accompanied by music, for the stimulus of movement provides a complete experience in itself. Nevertheless, it would be equally one-sided consciously to avoid altogether the practice of using music to inspire and accompany dance.

Among the many musical forms available, the suite, theme and variations, divertimenti, and programme music are suitable as dance accompaniment. Each of these forms usually consists of several short sections. Short pieces are particularly useful since it is a good plan to complete the dance in a single lesson.

If the music selected is primarily rhythmic it will usually be a suitable stimulus and accompaniment for stepping and jumping dances. This type of music will set one's feet tapping. If the music is primarily melodic it may stimulate lyrical dances characterised by gesture, contraction, extension and smooth travelling. Programme music because of its dramatic contrasts may stimulate dance in which there are contrasting dynamics.

The eight to twelve age groups will respond well to music which is lively and rhythmic and therefore stimulates action, whereas the older age groups will work well to music which is marked by definite changes in mood. Programme music is suitable for both age groups provided it is emotionally manageable. Epic film music for example is often too overpowering for dance. It requires mass movement reactions on a scale too vast for the classroom or hall. Schumann's *Scenes of Childhood* is an example of a piece of programme music on a more manageable scale.

Music may be used as a stimulus and an accompaniment for an activity or a structured dance. For example, after working on stepping, the teacher may say, 'Let me see you stepping when the music begins'. This is an example of using music as an accompaniment for an activity.

It is an advantage to have the music on tape so that any phrase may be cued precisely and any part of the music may be quickly returned to for movement repetition.

The choice of stimulus

In the long run the stimulus that sets the teacher's imagination on fire and brings a keen urge to begin exploration with a class is the one that is most likely to be productive. In this situation the class will be likely to catch the teacher's enthusiasm and the teacher himself will be in a motivated state of mind conducive to ingenuity in finding ways of interesting, and guiding the class. It is good to develop a flexible approach since the class may reject the teacher's ideas and in this event the teacher will be required to adapt quickly to the directions suggested by the children's response. Children are unconsciously the best judges of the suitability of material for them and when they do not respond well to material it is often an indication to the teacher that he must develop the lesson in another direction.

SUMMARY

1. Important principles of composition which the teacher bears in mind when observing and guiding children's work are:

(*a*) Repetition
(*b*) Sequence
(*c*) Climax.

2. From the vast range of possible subject matter for making dances the following have been considered: movement, literature, the world of nature, ritual, and voice sound and music. The richest source of all is movement and Chapter 2 deals with this subject matter. The subject matter which fires the imagination of the teacher will often be the most effective for the enthusiasm of the teacher will communicate to the children. Lastly, no matter how keen the teacher may be to work with the class on a theme, he must be flexible enough in approach to adapt his material if the children reject it.

FURTHER READING

Langer (22): Teachers undertaking project work in connection with dance will find Chapters 6 and 7 and the Appendix constraining and revealing.

Bodmer (38): 'Dance Composition' is an article which every teacher interested in composing should read.

Russell (33): A list of records suitable for dance, with helpful notes on some records, is provided in the Appendix.

Jordan (13): Chapter 4 considers music in the dance lesson.

Sachs (35): Chapter 4 is an authoritative account of dance and music in an historical perspective.

Bibliography

1. Arnheim, Rudolf. *Towards a Psychology of Art* (Faber 1967)
2. Barrault, Jean-Louis. *Reflections on the Theatre* (Rockcliffe 1951)
3. Cassirer, Ernst. *The Philosophy of Symbolic Forms*, vol. 11 (Yale University Press, paperback, 1968)
4. De Zoete, Beryl. *Dance and Drama in Bali* (Faber 1963)
5. Ghiselin, Brewster. (ed.). *The Creative Process* (A Mentor Book, New English Library edition, London 1952)
6. Giedion-Welcker, Carola. *Contemporary Sculpture* (Faber 1960)
7. Grohmann, Will. *The Art of Henry Moore* (Thames & Hudson 1960)
8. Hammacher, A. M. *Barbara Hepworth* (Thames & Hudson 1968)
9. Higginson, J. H. *Changing Thought in Primary and Secondary Education* (Macmillan 1969)
10. Hutchinson, Ann. *Labanotation* (a Theatre Arts Book, available from Dance Notation Bureau, 8 East 12th St, New York, N.Y. 10003: revised and expanded ed., 1970)
11. James, P. (ed.). *Henry Moore on Sculpture* (Macdonald 1968)
12. James, William. *Psychology, Briefer Course* (Macmillan 1892)
13. Jordan, Diana. *Childhood and Movement* (Blackwell 1966)
14. Joseph, B. L. *Elizabethan Acting* (O.U.P. 1964)
15. Laban, Rudolf. *Choreutics* (Macdonald & Evans 1966)
16. Laban, Rudolf. *Mastery of Movement on the Stage* (Macdonald & Evans, 2nd ed., 1960)
17. Laban, Rudolf. *Modern Education Dance* (Macdonald & Evans, 2nd ed., 1963)
18. Laban, Rudolf, and Lawrence, F. C. *Effort* (Macdonald & Evans 1947)
19. Langer, Suzanne. *Feeling and Form* (Scribners, New York 1953, Lyceum ed. S.L. 122)
20. Langer, Suzanne. *Philosophy in a New Key* (Mentor 1951)
21. Langer, Suzanne. *Philosophic Sketches* (Mentor 1964)
22. Langer, Suzanne. *Problems of Art* (Scribners 1957, S.L. 35)
23. North, Marion. *An Introduction to Movement Study and Teaching* (Macdonald & Evans 1971)

24. Piaget, Jean. *Play, Dreams and Imitation in Childhood* (R.K.P. 1962)

25. Piaget, Jean. *The Child's Conception of the World* (R.K.P. 1929)

26. Preston-Dunlop, Valerie. *The Handbook for Modern Educational Dance* (Macdonald & Evans, 1963)

27. Preston-Dunlop, Valerie. *Practical Kinetography Laban* (Macdonald & Evans 1969)

28. Read, Herbert. *Arp* (Thames & Hudson 1968)

29. Read, Herbert. *Icon and Idea* (Schocken paperback, by arr. Harvard University Press 1969)

30. Read, Herbert. *Education Through Art* (Faber, 3rd ed. 1969)

31. Reeves, James. *The Merry-Go-Round* (ed. Kaye Webb, Penguin Reprint 1969)

32. Russell, Joan. *Creative Dance in the Primary School* (Macdonald & Evans 1965)

33. Russell, Joan. *Creative Dance in the Secondary School* (Macdonald & Evans 1969)

34. Russell, Joan. *Modern Dance in Education* (Macdonald & Evans 1958)

35. Sachs, Curt. *World History of the Dance* (Norton, New York 1963)

36. Yeats, William Butler. *Collected Poems* (Macmillan 1967)

37. North, Marion. *Personality Assessment Through Movement* (Macdonald & Evans 1972)

Magazines and Articles

38. Bodmer, Sylvia. *Dance Composition* (Laban Art of Movement Guild Magazine, Nos. 36 and 38)

39. Shipman, Martin D. *A Sociological Perspective of Dance* (lecture delivered to the Dance Section of the Association of Teachers in Colleges and Departments of Education, 1969)

Glossary

The intention of the glossary is to help the reader to a better comprehension of the terms listed as they appear in the context of the book and not to present a rigid set of definitions. Continuing experience and study requires a flexible vocabulary which is not resistant to change and adaption.

ATTITUDES. There are two possible attitudes towards the motion factors. In one the mover fights against the motion factors and in the other he indulges in the motion factors.

    1. *Fighting against* A resisting or withholding attitude towards the motion factors resulting in the effort elements of firm touch, directness, suddenness, and bound flow.

    2. *Indulging in* A yielding attitude towards the motion factors resulting in the effort elements of fine touch, indirectness, suddenness and free-flow.

BODILY ACTIONS. A general term referring to the activities of jumping, travelling, stepping, contraction and extension, twisting and turning and gesturing.

BOUND FLOW. An effort element experienced in careful and restrained movement of a controlled character which is easy to stop at any moment and revealing a fighting attitude to the motion factor of flow.

CENTRE OF GRAVITY. For the purposes of this text the centre of gravity refers to the upper region of the pelvic area.

CONTRACTION. A term used loosely in the text in referring to movement in which the extremities of the body draw in towards each other and the body centre. With a more exact usage this form may refer to movement.

    1. Where the extremity of a limb draws in towards its base, the joint where it joins the trunk.

    2. Where the extremities of the trunk are drawn together from the body centre so that the chest area and pelvic area tilt, from the

body centre hinge, towards each other. This kind of contraction may occur in front, at the side, in the back, or at the diagonal surfaces of the trunk.

DIRECTNESS. An effort element experienced in movement which cuts economically through the space with singleness of intent and revealing a fighting attitude to the motion factor of space.

EFFORT. A term referring to those inner impulses which are visible in behaviour as movement qualities or effort elements.

EFFORT ELEMENTS. Effort elements derive from attitudes of the moving person towards the motion factors of Weight, Space, Time and Flow (Rudolf Laban (15), p. 8).

EXPRESSIVE MOVEMENT. Expressive movement refers in the text to that movement which gives form to imagined feeling. In dance experiences, feeling may give rise to form and form may give rise to new experiences of feeling.

EXTENSION. In this bodily action part of a limb or the extremity of a limb moves away from the base, the joint where it joins the trunk. When the action is a whole body action the limbs move away from the body centre.

FINE TOUCH. An effort element experienced in light movement and revealing an indulging attitude to the motion factor of weight.

FIRM TOUCH. An effort element experienced in strong powerful movement of considerable tension, and revealing a fighting attitude to the motion factor of weight.

FREE FLOW. An effort element experienced in unrestrained movement of an abandoned character, difficult to stop at any moment and revealing an indulging attitude to the motion factor of flow.

FREE RHYTHM. That pattern of movement in which the end of one movement becomes the beginning of the next and in which the relaxation of one tension prepares for the rise of a succeeding tension.

HALF-STEP. A step from a closed position where the feet are together to an open position or a step from an open position to a closed position.

GESTURE. A bodily action referring to a movement of a free part of the body.

GUIDANCE. Guidance refers to a manner of gesturing where a surface of the limb moves against the air in the direction of the path of the movement (see Hutchinson (10), p. 463).

ILLUSION. Illusion refers in the text to the creation of an appearance or semblance in the act of dancing. In dancing the illusions of power, time, and space may be created.

INDIRECTNESS. An effort element experienced in movement which evolves in a pliant manner in space and revealing an indulging attitude to the motion factor of space.

INSIDE GUIDANCE. In this kind of gesture the inside surface of the arm moves against the air in the direction of the path of movement. The inside surface of the arm runs from the palm along the arm to the inside surface of the elbow and on to the armpit.

JUMPING. An action in which the body leaves the floor for a short time.

LEADING. Leading is a term used in connection with gesture when a part of the body initiates the bodily action/movement by moving ahead into the space (Hutchinson (10), p. 463).

LITTLE FINGER GUIDANCE. In this gesture the little finger edge surface of the arm moves against the air. The little finger edge surface of the arm extends from the little finger in a straight line to the shoulder when the arm is pressed against the side with the palm and inside surface of the elbow touching the side of the body.

METRIC RHYTHM. A term referring to a pattern of movement which may be measured against some kind of periodicity or beat.

MOTION FACTORS. A term referring to the Weight, Space, Time and Flow aspects of movement.

OUTSIDE GUIDANCE. In this kind of gesture the outside surface of the arm moves against the air. The outside surface extends from the back of the hand along the arm to the bony side of the elbow and on to the top of the shoulder.

SEQUENTIAL MOVEMENT (SUCCESSIVE FLOW) 'A sequential movement is one in which movement flows from one part of the body to another in succession, passing from joint to joint, or from vertebra to vertebra in the case of successions in the spine.' (Hutchinson (10), p. 456).

SIMULTANEOUS MOVEMENT FLOW In simultaneous movement flow the active parts begin moving at the same time and finish moving at the same time. In a whole body contraction from an extended position for example the head, arms, trunk and legs will begin moving at the same time and reach their destination at the same time.

STEPPING. Stepping is a bodily action consisting of a transference of the weight of the body and a leg gesture.

SUDDENNESS. An effort element experienced in swift, urgent movement of brief duration and revealing a fighting attitude to the motion factor of time.

SUSTAINMENT. An effort element experienced in leisurely unhurried movement which lingers and revealing an indulging attitude to the motion factor of time.

THUMB GUIDANCE. In this kind of gesture the thumb edge surface of the arm moves against the air. The thumb edge extends from the thumb in a straight line to the shoulder when the arm is against the side with the inside surface of the elbow and the palm touching the side of the body.

TRAVELLING. The form of stepping which results when the mover's concentration and emphasis is on the floor pathway and aerial pathway traced by the movement through the space.

TURNING. A rotating action of the whole body.

TWISTING. An action in which only a part of the body rotates, or an action in which two parts rotate in contrary directions about the same axis.

WHOLE STEP. A step from one open position to another as in normal walking. In this action one foot passes by the other.

ZONES. A spatial division according to the structure of the body so that there is an arm zone, a leg zone, and a trunk zone. Each zone is the area in space within normal reach of that body part.

Index

accents, 83, 84
accompaniment, 28, 75, 92–5
action(s), contracting and extending, 25,
    26, 45, 46, 62
    dynamic, 36
    gesture, 28, 29, 30
    jumping, 26, 27, 61
    rhythmic phrases of, 24
    stepping, 24, 25
    travelling, 24
    turning, 27
    twisting, 28, 29
adolescents, 11, 12, 22
architecture, 18
Armitage, Kenneth, 51
Arp, Jean, 54
attitudes, to flow, 24, 37
    to space, 39
    to time, 19, 38, 39
    to weight, 37

Bodmer, Sylvia, 97
body, centre, 25, 26, 45
    parts of, 28–30
    shape, 24, 32, 33, 50–2

Cassirer, Ernst, 13
centre, body, 25, 26, 45, 46
children, characteristics of, 11, 26, 31
    Middle School, 11, 21
    subjective insight of, 20, 22
clarity and mastery, 74
    repetition, 75
    timing, 74
class, the, 24, 25
    dance background for composition,
    34
communication, 20
composition, 82–9
conceptual value, 22
creativity, 73, 74, 75

cummings, e. e., 89

dance, accompaniment, 28, 75, 92–6
    characterisation, 89, 90, 91
    composition(s), 82–9, examples, 84–
    88
    court, 30
    educational value of, 20, 22, 36
    gesture, 31, 32
    the lesson, 76–81
    mode of meaning, 20
    prancing and dancing, 12
    significance of, 12–15
    social value of, 36, 67
    stimuli, 88–92
    subject matter, 24–69, 88–92
dance drama, 88–92
development, in organising the syllabus,
    69–72
De Zoete, Beryl, 14, 18, 19, 21, 54, 75
drawing, 15, 54
dynamics, 15–17, 36–44

education, aim of dance in, 20, 22, 36
effort, 36–44, 101,
    moods, 36
elevation, 26, 27
Eliot, T. S., 90
emotions, 36
energies, 13

floor work, 30, 32, 33, 46, 47
fluency, 31

gesture, 28–32
Giedion-Welcker, Carola, 51, 52
group work, 56–69,
    interplay, 91

half-steps, 24, 25
Hutchinson, Ann, 101, 102

illusion, 12–20
import, 12, 20
improvisation, 20

James, William, 25
Jordan, Diana, 23, 97

Klee, Paul, 54
knowledge, 20

Laban, Rudolph, 15, 16, 36, 101
labile, 52, 53
Langer, Susanne, 14, 23, 97
Lear, Edward, 56
lesson, the, 76–81
Lewis, C. S., 89

Masefield, John, 88
Michaelangelo, 33
Middle School, 21, 22
mind (see import)
mobility (see labile)
mood, 36
motion factors, 24, 37–9
movement, dance movement, 12
    everyday movement and dance move-
        ment, 15
    expression, 13
    ideas, Chap. 2
    observation of, 74
Moore, Henry, 33, 50, 51
music, 95, 96

North, Marion, 23, 36, 44, 56, 69, 81

observation, 74
orientation, 45–8, 52–4

partner work, 47, 48, 57, 58, 60
pathways, 53, 54
percussion, 75, 94
poetry, 88, 89
Preston-Dunlop, Valerie, 36, 44, 56
progress, 31, 39

Read, Herbert, 13, 14, 22, 23
repetition, 82, 83
rhythm, 29, 83, 84
ritual, 92
Rodin, 33
Russell, Joan, 23, 36, 44, 56, 73, 74, 81,
    97

Sachs, Curt, 13, 61, 97
scale, 49
sculpture, 32
shape, 24, 32, 33, 50, 51, 52
Shipman, Martin, 67
space, 17, 18, 19, 44–56
subjective life, 13
stable, 33, 52
stance, 32, 52, 53
stillness, 24, 32, 33, 50
stimuli, 88–92, 96
symbolic forms, 13

teacher, the, 73–82
time, illusion, 19

voice sound, 75, 92, 93, 94

walking, 33, 34
whole-steps, 24, 25

Yeats, William Butler, 88

zones, 48, 49